JACK MAXWELL AND JOE TOMLINSON

WITH A FOREWORD
BY CATHERINE O'REGAN

EXPERIMENTS IN AUTOMATING IMMIGRATION SYSTEMS

BRISTOL
UNIVERSITY
PRESS

First published in Great Britain in 2022 by

Bristol University Press
University of Bristol
1–9 Old Park Hill
Bristol
BS2 8BB
UK
t: +44 (0)117 954 5940
e: bup-info@bristol.ac.uk

Details of international sales and distribution partners are available at
bristoluniversitypress.co.uk

British Library Cataloguing in Publication Data
A catalogue record for this book is available from the British Library

ISBN 978-1-5292-1984-5 hardcover
ISBN 978-1-5292-1985-2 ePub
ISBN 978-1-5292-1986-9 ePdf

Cover design: Liam Roberts
Front cover image: iStock/Vadim Sazhniev

Jack dedicates this book to Sammy.

Joe dedicates this book to his parents, Jeff and Julie.

Contents

Acknowledgements

This book emerged out of our work together, across a number of years, seeking to understand and respond to the impacts of automated systems in the public sector. Throughout that time, we benefited from the input and support of the entire Public Law Project team, and we would particularly like to thank Jo Hickman, Director of PLP, for supporting us to develop work in this area. We have also benefited from discussions with many friends and colleagues similarly interested in automated systems in the public sector. There are too many to mention here but we would like to express particular thanks to Swee Leng Harris, Ben Jaffey QC, Jennifer Cobbe, Ravi Naik, Chris Knight, Reuben Binns, Cori Crider, Oliver Butler, Robert Thomas, Jeremias Adams-Prassl, Adam Harkens, Christiaan van Veen, and Crofton Black for many stimulating conversations and comments on various drafts. We also benefited immensely from a roundtable discussion at the Bonavero Institute of Human Rights at the University of Oxford on 'Judicial Review in a Digital Age', co-hosted with Liberty, Oliver Butler, and Catherine O'Regan. Finally, we would like to thank the wonderful team at Bristol University Press who have been friendly and diligent while supporting us throughout.

Foreword

Digital technology holds out considerable promise as a tool for speedy and cost-effective decision making in many areas in the public sector, yet it holds out challenges as well. In modern democracies, we expect public sector decision making to be accountable and fair. Parliament should play a key role in ensuring accountability and fairness in public sector decision making, not only through its role as legislator, in which it structures the rules to be applied and processes to be followed, but also in the role it plays in scrutinizing the conduct of the executive and civil service. In addition, courts and tribunals should serve as key mechanisms to ensure accountability and fairness. Policy makers and public lawyers are only just beginning to think about how these traditional mechanisms may need to adapt to ensure accountability and fairness in the digital age.

This book makes an important contribution to that discussion. It provides three case studies of the use of automated decision making in the field of immigration in the United Kingdom. The case studies provide clear illustrations of the challenges that the digital age presents for existing mechanisms of accountability and fairness. The challenges are, perhaps, particularly acute in the field of immigration, the focus of this book, given that immigrants are not citizens, and have limited, if any, influence in democratic politics. Moreover, where immigration has become a contentious political issue, as it has in the UK, mechanisms to ensure fairness and accountability may be at risk of attenuation in the political process. Indeed, the case study on the EU (European Union) Settlement Scheme illustrates how other political issues may affect the design of suitable mechanisms of accountability. The question of whether a tribunal appeal would be afforded to aggrieved applicants under the scheme was an issue in the overall withdrawal negotiations, with the UK adopting the approach that if a withdrawal agreement was not reached with the EU, aggrieved applicants under the scheme would not be afforded a right of appeal to a tribunal. Because an agreement with the EU was reached, a right of appeal to a tribunal was afforded.

Leaving aside the challenge posed by immigration, this book illustrates the challenges that automated decision making will raise across the field of public sector decision making. Examples include the problem of automation bias (the fact that automated decisions tend to be accepted as correct without analysis), the opaqueness of automated decision making (sometimes because of technological complexity and sometimes because software developers refuse to provide explanations on grounds of commercial confidentiality), the lack of expertise in the judiciary to assess and analyse automated decision making, and the problem of incomplete, skewed or bad data, which results in automated decision making reproducing discriminatory patterns or simply making bad decisions. In thinking about how to ensure accountability and fairness in public sector decision making in the digital age, all these problems will have to be addressed.

An important part of the solution to these challenges, it would seem, would be for government to develop a protocol to guide the use of automated decision making tools to ensure that they are subjected to sufficient pre-application use to avoid obvious shortcomings. As the Committee on Standards in Public Life recently recommended, '[g]overnment needs to identify and embed authoritative ethical principles and issue accessible guidance on AI governance to those using it in the public sector. Government and regulators must also establish a coherent regulatory framework that sets clear legal boundaries on how AI should be used in the public sector'.[1] Such a framework would guide the adoption of automated decision making software and would serve, at least in part, to fulfil the duty to act fairly that public sector decision makers bear. It would be an important first step in ensuring that mechanisms of accountability and fairness function effectively in the digital age.

But thought will need to be given as well to forms of administrative law remedy in this field. The book also considers the relative merits and weakness of tribunal appeals and judicial review in the field of automated decision making, particularly in the first case study, relating to the use of voice recognition software to identify fraud in visa application processes. The issues raised by that case study indicate that the question of effective remedies for those aggrieved by automated public decision making requires investigation across the field of public sector decision making.

This book, therefore, provides a timely and useful analysis of the challenges that need to be addressed to ensure automated decision making is accountable and fair. It should be read widely by politicians, policy makers, civil servants, judges, and public lawyers as well as scholars in the fields of public administration, political science, and law. Understanding the nature of the problem must be the first step to solving it, and this book contributes significantly to that understanding.

Catherine O'Regan
Professor of Human Rights Law
Director of the Bonavero Institute of Human Rights
University of Oxford
July 2021

ONE

The Home Office Laboratory

The Home Office – the main UK public authority responsible for immigration – is keenly interested in identifying 'sham' marriages which are designed to game the immigration system.[1] Since at least 2015, the department has used an automated system to determine whether to investigate a proposed marriage.[2] Marriage registrars across the country transmit details of proposed marriages to the system via 'data feeds'. The system applies eight 'risk factors' to assess the risk that a couple's marriage is a sham. These risk factors include the couple's interactions before the registrar, 'shared travel events', and age difference. The system allocates couples either a 'green' rating, indicating that no investigation is warranted, or a 'red' rating, indicating that an investigation is warranted to identify possible 'sham activity'. This algorithm processes a large number of marriages each year. In a 12-month period across 2019 and 2020, the Home Office received 16,600 notifications of marriages involving a non-European national, of which 1,299 were subsequently investigated.[3] These investigations can have a range of adverse consequences for individuals and their families, and they inevitably reach into the most private aspects of people's lives in a manner that can be 'gruelling'.[4] There have been recent reports of wedding ceremonies being interrupted so that officials can question people about their sex lives, an official finding a nude photograph on a person's phone and showing it to others in the room, and dawn raids being carried out to check if couples are sharing a bed.[5] We know little about how this automated system works, its impacts on those processed by it, and how effective it has been in successfully detecting sham marriages. This example of automation's growing role in government immigration systems is not unique. In fact, it is being replicated in many different corners of the Home Office immigration bureaucracy.[6] The Home Office is currently one of the largest purchasers of IT services in government.[7] The government's 2025 border strategy promises a 'border ecosystem' where '[a]ccurate data is gathered efficiently and shared across government at scale', thereby 'maximising data driven, automated decision making'.[8] Why is this happening?

Frontline immigration decision making is a tough job.[9] It requires busy officials to apply complex law and policy.[10] Immigration policy has been the subject of intense political pressure for decades, with 'system overhauls' and changes to law and policy flowing almost endlessly. Immigration law has become so complex that, in 2017, the Home Office asked the Law Commission – the independent statutory body charged with reviewing the law of England and Wales – to examine the problem and see what could be done to simplify the rules.[11] Alongside keeping up with and applying Byzantine law and policy, officials must also assess applications that are often factually complex and emotionally charged – from making decisions about the *bona fides* of businesses to assessing the credibility of human trafficking and torture survivors. The evidence presented by applicants varies, but the supporting materials are often far from complete for a range of reasons.[12] Home Office decision making is not a court-like process where the details of claims and supporting evidence are thrashed out fully. Decisions generally have to be made quickly to avoid an unmanageable backlog. In this high-volume environment, the basic aim is for decisions to be made efficiently and accurately.[13] The Home Office often succeeds at this job, too: producing vast numbers of accurate decisions that allow people to lawfully change their immigration status. But, within a bureaucracy like this, errors are inevitably made, both in individual cases and at a systemic level. One does not need to look far for failures of immigration decision making causing anything from delay to severe human suffering.[14]

As the capacity and availability of digital technology increased, it was almost inevitable that the Home Office would start to reach for automated systems to support or even replace the decision making of human officials.[15] These systems came with promises of quicker, cheaper, more consistent, and more effective decision making. In simple terms, this shift held the potential to ease the significant decision-making burden on the department. But it was not just the promises of automation itself that were tempting. The UK government had growing confidence in the public sector's capacity to use technology successfully, too. Historically, large public sector IT projects have routinely failed or disappointed, leading to the UK being widely perceived as 'ground zero' for failed e-government projects.[16] However, following the creation of the Government Digital Service in 2011, the UK is now widely considered to be a global leader in digital public services.[17] Public bodies in the UK have increasingly turned to automated solutions, including for welfare services and justice systems.[18] Similarly, other countries are starting to automate parts of their bureaucratic systems, including their immigration systems.[19] From the Home Office's perspective, the question is not 'should we automate?' but 'why *not* automate?'[20]

Government immigration systems are now in a state of transition. Automation is being developed and deployed in many systems. It is also moving from 'back room' processing systems to become a significant part of the citizen–state interaction and decision making itself. At the same time, the risks of automating government decision making are now starting to come to the surface. In the UK, the most high-profile episode to date involved education, rather than immigration, when the government decided, after cancelling exams due to the COVID-19 pandemic, to provide students with grades based on an algorithm.[21] Once grades were released, it became apparent that the algorithm had, based on historical school performance data, downgraded about 40 per cent of the exam results predicted by teachers. This led to public outrage and protests, which ultimately saw the government abandon the algorithm and the Prime Minister, Boris Johnson, seek cover by suggesting to affected students that their grades 'were almost derailed by a mutant algorithm'.[22] The responsible minister survived the debacle, but several senior officials were sacked, and the algorithm was ditched for the following year's exams.[23]

While the injustices of automated decision making occasionally pierce public consciousness and prompt backlash and debate, much automation – and its capacity to generate injustice – does not. Instead, it is hidden from view – even for those who are actively looking for it.[24] This is certainly the case for much of the automation within the Home Office. The shift to automated systems has not, to this point, prompted changes to the law or attracted much political or public debate. Most people subject to automated systems will not even be aware they have been processed by such a system.

In this book, we explore how the Home Office has started to experiment with automated systems, with significant consequences for individuals and their families, as well as wider society and the economy. For the people affected, the results of these experiments have ranged from quicker processing times and less stress to loss of immigration status and even deportation. Ultimately, we suggest that the Home Office is engaging in *risky* experimentation with automated systems. If these systems are to be rolled out further, we argue that a precautionary approach is essential.

We examine three Home Office systems which, through various means, have come into public view. The first is an automated voice recognition system used to detect English language testing fraud. The second is the EU Settlement Scheme, which was set up after the Brexit vote to register over four million EU citizens resident in the UK and relies on vast automated data sharing between government departments. The third is an algorithm for streaming visa applications, which discriminated on the grounds of nationality and race. We are conscious that these three systems represent merely the tip of the iceberg: these types of systems are already widely used in the immigration system, and their use is set to expand even further in future.[25] Further investigation and analysis of automated immigration systems will be crucial in the coming years. Indeed, we hope our book prompts and contributes to those endeavours.

The use of automated systems in government can be analysed profitably from a range of perspectives. Our primary concern in this book is administrative justice: how justice (or injustice) is realized through public decision making about individuals and the redress mechanisms by which people can challenge those decisions.[26] We do not address the substantive merits of the government's immigration policies, but instead focus on the government's capacity to implement those policies efficiently while ensuring justice for individuals. To do this, we focus on three dimensions of the automated systems we examine.[27] First, we consider what can be called the 'rules' – the law and guidance underpinning the system, and how they frame its development and use. Second, we look at 'decision making' – how the state makes initial contact with citizens and how it reaches decisions in particular cases. This is the territory where automation is most directly encroaching. Third, we examine 'redress' – the mechanisms available to challenge decisions, how they have or have not been used, and how effective they have been in dealing with problems of automation. It is by exploring these dimensions in respect of the three systems we examine that we show a pattern of risky experimentation with automated systems in the Home Office, and argue that a precautionary approach to the development and use of these systems is now required.

TWO

Testing Systems

At dawn on 30 June 2014, Raja Noman Hussain awoke to find about 15 immigration and police officers raiding his house.[1] Raja, a 22-year-old Pakistani man, had arrived in the UK several years earlier to study. Now he was being accused of cheating in an English language proficiency test approved by the Home Office, which he had sat in 2012 to meet a condition of his visa. After confirming his ID, the officers told him to grab some clothes, handcuffed him, and took him into immigration detention. Raja spent the next four months in detention, during which time he estimates he met over 100 other international students who had also been detained on the same basis. What followed was six years of legal battles over the cheating allegation, which disrupted his studies, estranged him from his family, and cost him around £30,000. Finally, in early 2021, Raja succeeded in clearing his name and confirming his right to be in the UK.

Raja was one of the tens of thousands of students whose visas were revoked or curtailed – and studies disrupted or ended – after the Home Office accused them of cheating in a government-approved English language test. This scandal eventually hit the headlines. The ensuing appeals and judicial reviews – which became known as the 'ETS cases' – have cost the government millions of pounds.[2] What is less appreciated about this debacle is that much of it centred on a failed automated system: a voice recognition algorithm which the government used to identify suspected cheats. This chapter explores that side of the story.

The scandal unfolds

English language requirements have long formed part of UK immigration law.[3] A 1914 law required that an 'alien' applying for citizenship prove that 'he is of good character and has an adequate knowledge of the English language'.[4] Since 2007, successive governments extended English language requirements to other types of immigration status: indefinite leave to remain, family visas, work visas, student visas, and so on. These requirements were said to serve the dual purposes of ensuring that migrants could work, study, and live successfully in the UK,[5] while reducing the numbers of migrants overall.[6] English language skills are now a requirement for most long-term visas and for settlement.[7]

For some people, it is relatively easy to prove that they can speak English. For example, they can do so by being a national of a majority English-speaking country or having completed a degree taught in English. For others, the only option is to sit an approved test. The government enlists private companies to develop and administer these tests, rather than doing so itself. In April 2011, following a tender process, the government licensed six companies to provide English language tests to immigrants to the UK.

One of those companies was Educational Testing Service (ETS). Based in the US, ETS is one of the largest private educational testing organizations in the world. One of the tests provided by ETS is the Test of English for International Communication (TOEIC), a multi-part test of listening, reading, speaking, and writing skills. At the time, the reading and writing parts of the TOEIC were completed on paper. For the spoken part, candidates were recorded reading a text aloud. ETS administered the TOEIC around the world via local, third-party contractors. ETS developed the test, the contractors registered candidates, ran the test centres, and administered the test, and the tests were then sent to ETS to be marked.

Between 2011 and 2014, over 58,000 people sat the TOEIC at dozens of test centres across the UK.[8] In February 2014, the BBC revealed evidence of cheating at two TOEIC test centres, particularly by overseas students.[9] It broadcast footage of people paying money to intermediaries to ensure they passed the test, and examiners giving candidates the answers and allowing proxy test-takers to complete the spoken and written parts of the test. This placed the Home Office in a quandary. Theresa May MP, then Home Secretary, had spoken out strongly about 'tightening the rules' on English language requirements and 'cracking down on bogus colleges [and] bogus students'.[10] But the BBC's revelations raised serious questions about the credibility of the system the government had established.

The government's response to the BBC's revelations was shaped by three important assumptions.[11] The first assumption was that the TOEIC cheating was systematic and widespread. It was seen as implicating potentially tens of thousands of tests and demanding a response on a similar scale. The second assumption was that the response had to be, in the words of departmental officials, 'robust' and 'vigorous'. The government could not simply chalk up the TOEIC cheating as a systemic failing and take steps to prevent it from happening again. It had to go after the people and organizations involved. As Sir Philip Rutnam, then Permanent Secretary at the Home Office, later described it, the government was set on 'finding the criminals, closing down bogus colleges and dealing with people whom we had evidence to suggest had their immigration status here on the basis of deception'.[12] The third assumption was that this response had to be speedy. The government was determined to act on the cheating as soon as possible.

These three assumptions complicated the government's task. How could it quickly assess tens of thousands of TOEIC tests going back almost three years for evidence of fraud? In March 2014, ETS proposed a solution to this problem: it would use an automated voice recognition system to determine which people had cheated on the TOEIC. This was novel: ETS had never before used voice recognition software to identify cheating on the TOEIC.[13]

The automated voice recognition process had three steps. First, ETS's voice recognition system analysed the audio recordings of the speaking portion of each test. The system flagged cases in which the same person appeared to have spoken in multiple tests and might thus be a paid proxy. Of the 58,000 tests taken in the UK between 2011 and 2014, the system flagged about 98 per cent as cases of cheating. Second, the flagged recordings were reviewed manually by two human 'checkers'. If both checkers confirmed the system's decision, the person's results were marked 'invalid'. If there remained some doubt, the results were marked 'questionable'. The checkers confirmed the system's decision in about 58 per cent of cases and expressed some doubt about the remaining 42 per cent. Third, ETS reclassified some cases after reviewing the overall patterns for each test centre. For example, if a person had taken their test at a centre where the system had flagged numerous other invalid results, ETS might also invalidate that person's results. This was an automated process with many humans 'in the loop'. ETS concluded that 97 per cent of UK tests taken between 2011 and 2014 – over 56,000 tests – were invalid or questionable.

The Home Office matched the ETS evidence against its own records in a spreadsheet called the 'Lookup Tool', and then used it to take action against tens of thousands of students. Under immigration law, the Home Office has a range of powers to cancel or revoke a person's leave to remain in the UK, or refuse a pending application, if it is tainted by deception.[14] For students with invalid TOEIC results, the Home Office cancelled their visas and refused any pending applications. Some were stopped at airports as they tried to enter the UK. Others were taken into immigration detention in the UK and subsequently deported. For students with questionable results, the Home Office generally required them to sit another test and attend an interview, although some appear to have been subject to immigration enforcement, too.[15] Estimates vary as to the precise number of people subject to action based on alleged TOEIC cheating. The National Audit Office puts the figure at 25,000 people;[16] the House of Commons Library at over 35,000;[17] and the Court of Appeal, in one judgment, at over 40,000.[18]

Three big mistakes

The ETS cases are a clear example of automated decision making infiltrating an immigration system, with serious consequences for the people affected. The Home Office's decision making in these cases was riddled with errors and oversights. Three mistakes were particularly significant: the initial decision to use ETS's voice recognition system; the failure to appreciate the problems with the evidence it produced; and the use of that evidence to make decisions in particular cases.

The first big mistake concerned the Home Office's initial decision to use ETS's voice recognition system. When the government proposes to automate some part of its decision making, it confronts a basic issue: is the automated system suitable for the task? This depends on, among other things, whether the system generally produces the right answer, in light of the task assigned to it and the relevant legal context, and whether the risk of a wrong answer is fairly distributed among different groups. Governments around the world are beginning to develop frameworks to help them ask and answer these questions.[19] The Canadian government has been a leader in this area.[20] It requires agencies to go through a rigorous process before developing or deploying an automated system. This includes assessing the risks posed by the system, monitoring the system's outcomes, getting an independent expert review of the system, and ensuring that the data collected for the system are relevant, accurate and current.

The Home Office's decision making in the ETS cases lies at the other end of the spectrum. Neither the Home Office nor

ETS had ever used this technology before to detect cheating on the TOEIC.[21] Yet the Home Office took no meaningful steps to confirm that the ETS system was accurate before deciding to use it. In June 2014, it sent a small delegation to the ETS headquarters in the US, to learn about the system and listen to a sample of recordings.[22] But none of the people in the delegation had any expertise in voice recognition or speech analysis, and in any case ETS refused to disclose any details about its system because of commercial confidentiality.[23] The delegation simply relied on ETS's claims that the technology was fit for purpose. The Upper Tribunal later found that the delegation 'accepted uncritically everything reported by ETS'.[24]

In August 2014, the Home Office convened a secret meeting of technical experts in the UK, to discuss whether the ETS evidence could support criminal prosecutions of fraudulent colleges and proxy test-takers. According to one attendee, the experts raised a 'great big raft of very very technical questions' at the meeting, which would need to be answered before they could determine the reliability of the evidence.[25] But the Home Office did not address those questions or commission an independent review into the ETS evidence. It simply continued to rely on it to cancel visas and remove people from the UK. It was not until February 2016 that the Home Office sought any independent expert assurance about the ETS evidence.[26] The Home Office's decision to use ETS's voice recognition system rested solely on ETS's own assurances. It assumed that this novel technology provided a sound basis for decision making. Had the Home Office looked a bit closer, however, it might have realized that the ETS evidence raised more questions than it answered.

The second big mistake was that the Home Office failed to appreciate the problems with the accuracy of the ETS evidence. Broadly speaking, the accuracy of a voice recognition system is a function of the quality of the system (that is, its capacity to correctly identify a particular voice from given recordings), and the quality of its inputs (that is, the length, clarity, and integrity of the audio recordings fed into the system). The ETS evidence suffered from significant problems in both of these respects.

ETS claimed that its voice recognition system had an error rate of less than 2 per cent. This figure was derived from a pilot conducted in 2012 and 2013 using recordings from a different test: the Test of English as a Foreign Language (TOEFL).[27] But there were two issues with this pilot figure of 2 per cent. First, ETS did not specify whether it measured false positives or false negatives. A false positive would occur where the system incorrectly accused someone of using a proxy test-taker, while a false negative would occur where the system incorrectly failed to identify someone who had used a proxy test-taker. In designing any automated system there is generally an unavoidable trade-off between these two types of error: if a system is adjusted to produce fewer false negatives, it will generally also produce more false positives. In different contexts, one type of error may be more significant than the other. In screening people for a serious disease, for instance, it may be more important to avoid false negatives, to ensure that as many people as possible who have the disease receive treatment. In the criminal justice system, however, it may be more important to avoid false positives, to avoid punishing any innocent people, even at the cost of letting off some guilty people. The ETS cases seem to fall into the latter category. The grave consequences of falsely accusing someone of TOEIC fraud significantly outweigh the consequences of failing to identify all of the people who cheated. But the pilot figure shed little light on the accuracy of ETS's voice recognition system, or whether it struck an appropriate balance between these different types of errors.

ETS also did not keep records of the quality of the TOEFL audio recordings used in the pilot, or the quality of the TOEIC audio recordings it analysed for the Home Office.[28] The trial figure could only be confidently applied to the ETS evidence if there was some parity between the quality of these two sets of recordings. If the TOEIC recordings were much lower quality than the TOEFL recordings, the error rate for the ETS evidence might be much higher than 2 per cent. The pilot was, therefore, of limited use in assessing the accuracy of the ETS evidence.[29]

In light of these issues, several experts expressed doubts about the ETS evidence in 2015 and 2016. Philip Harrison, an expert briefed on behalf of several students accused of cheating, concluded that it was simply impossible to determine the reliability of the ETS evidence and the likely number of false positives.[30] Peter French, one of the Home Office's experts, agreed that the number of false positives generated by the voice recognition system 'cannot be estimated with any great degree of precision'.[31] However, French concluded that '[i]f the 2% error rate established for the TOEFL pilot recordings were to apply to the TOEIC recordings, then I would estimate the rate of false positives to be very substantially less than 1% after the process of assessment by trained listeners had been applied'.[32] The Home Office has relied heavily on this 1 per cent figure to justify its handling of the ETS cases, both in public and before the courts.[33] When defending the Home Office's actions before the House of Commons Public Accounts Committee in 2019, Sir Philip Rutnam asserted that:

> [T]he Department's view throughout has been that the risk of people being wrongly caught up in this is very small. ... [T]he level of false matches, according to Professor French, who is the leading expert in this field, is likely to be in the region of no more than 1%.[34]

But the 1 per cent figure was based on several important assumptions. The first assumption, evident in the excerpt from French's evidence, was that the pilot figure of 2 per cent could be applied to the ETS evidence. This assumption was dubious. The second assumption, as French noted publicly in 2019, concerned the integrity of the inputs: the TOEIC audio recordings.[35] ETS and the Home Office assumed that, if a recording was of someone other than the person supposed to have sat the test, the person had cheated. But if the recordings had been confused or manipulated at some stage between the person taking the test and the analysis by ETS, this assumption was also unsound.

As people began challenging their treatment by the Home Office, real doubts emerged about the integrity of the TOEIC recordings. A joint report by experts for both sides in July 2016 pointed out numerous issues.[36] There were no data available to identify the time, date, and location of each recording. There were no audit trails recording the chain of storage, processing, and transfer of the recordings from the test centres in the UK to ETS headquarters in the US. There was no identifying link between a particular audio file and a particular person (e.g. in a filename or description). Most importantly, all of ETS's procedures for preserving the integrity of the recordings depended on the reliability of the test centre staff. But the Home Office knew that at least some of the test centres had participated in, or even orchestrated, the cheating uncovered by the BBC.[37] Any assumption as to their reliability was therefore highly questionable. Peter Sommer, one of the experts, concluded that it was 'unsafe' for the Home Office to rely on the recordings as the basis of its decisions.[38]

The various doubts about the accuracy of the ETS evidence are reflected in the Home Office's 'Lookup Tool', the spreadsheet that matched the evidence against the Home Office's records. The tool contained numerous apparent errors. It included people who had no need to take the TOEIC, as a matter of immigration law, and denied ever doing so.[39] It included people who had failed their tests, even though they had ostensibly paid someone else to sit them.[40] It misstated people's nationalities, including misdescribing people as British nationals, who would have had no need to take the TOEIC.[41] It stated that people cheated on two different TOEIC tests held on the same day but in different locations.[42] It also stated that people took their test at particular times and places, when there was objective evidence (e.g. receipts) showing that they were elsewhere at that time.[43]

In short, there is no way to determine how many students ETS wrongly identified as having cheated on their TOEIC test. The National Audit Office concluded in 2019 that:

> It is difficult to estimate accurately how many innocent people may have been wrongly identified as cheating. Voice recognition technology is new, and it had not been used before with TOEIC tests. The degree of error is difficult to determine accurately because there was no piloting or control group established for TOEIC tests.[44]

The Home Office's reliance on the 1 per cent figure was, and continues to be, unsustainable. As the UK Statistics Authority, the independent statistics regulator, observed in 2019, there is 'considerable uncertainty' around the 1 per cent figure, which 'has not always been conveyed clearly' by the Home Office.[45]

It is important to note that the two mistakes discussed are closely connected. Because the Home Office failed to take any meaningful steps to confirm that the ETS evidence was accurate, it was either unaware of or unconcerned about the serious shortcomings of that evidence. But it might still have been possible for the Home Office to mitigate those flaws in its decision making in particular cases.

This brings us to a third big mistake: the Home Office's use of the ETS evidence in particular cases. Where a public official uses an automated system to help them make a decision, the interaction between the official and the system can go wrong in at least two ways.[46] The first risk is that an official might fail to detect that the system has made an error in performing the task assigned to it. If the official then relies on the erroneous output, this is likely to lead to a poor or unlawful decision. This risk is magnified by the phenomenon of automation bias: the tendency for people to rely uncritically on the outputs of automated systems, rather than meaningfully scrutinizing them. The second risk is that the official might not appreciate that, even when the system performs correctly, it does not incorporate all of the factors that they are required to consider in making a decision. If the official relies solely on the system's outputs, rather than considering all of the relevant circumstances, this may also lead to a poor or unlawful decision.

The ETS cases illustrate both of these failings. The Home Office was not in a position to assess whether ETS had made a mistake in concluding that the same person had spoken in multiple tests. It did not ask ETS for the underlying recordings and ETS declined to disclose its voice recognition system.[47] Other than reviewing the data for obvious errors and duplicates, the Home Office simply trusted that ETS's system had produced accurate results.[48] At the same time, Home Office officials were wholly reliant on the ETS evidence. They did not turn their minds to the broader question of whether, in all the circumstances, a person had cheated on their test. In most individual cases, the Home Office was entirely dependent on the information provided by ETS.[49] This was not a case of solely automated decision making, where a decision is taken by an automated system without any human involvement in a particular case. Two human checkers were interposed between ETS's voice recognition system and the Home Office. These checkers appeared willing to disagree with the system's outputs: they expressed doubt about them in about 42 per cent of cases.[50] But the ETS evidence was necessarily limited to whether the same person appeared to have spoken in multiple tests. It could not, and did not, consider all of the circumstances and, in particular, any other corroborating or contradictory evidence. The Upper Tribunal's decision in the case of *AB* highlights the problems with this approach.[51] The Home Secretary had refused AB's application for leave to remain, on the ground of suspected TOEIC fraud. But it emerged that AB's husband had orchestrated the fraud, as part of his controlling and abusive behaviour toward her. The Upper Tribunal allowed the appeal, holding that the Home Secretary should have granted AB's application.

When presented with the unreliable ETS evidence, the Home Office not only failed to scrutinize it, but relied wholly on it to make decisions. In using this evidence on such a large scale, the Home Office ran the risk of taking action against thousands of innocent students. As the House of Commons Public Accounts Committee concluded in 2019, the Home Office 'rushed to penalise students without establishing whether ETS was involved in fraud or if it had reliable evidence of people cheating'.[52] Such action had grave consequences for the reputations, livelihoods, and futures of the people involved.

Mildly astonishing opacity

Automated government decisions are often opaque, in the sense that it is difficult for a person outside government to know how or why the decision has been reached.[53] There can be a range of reasons for this opacity.[54] The government might deliberately withhold information about its automated systems, to prevent people from gaming the system or to protect the commercial information of its private sector suppliers. Opacity may also be the result of poor record-keeping. Without accurate records about a system – covering not just the system's technical details, but the broader social and technical context for its design, development and use – it may be very difficult to understand how it works and whether it meets legal and governance standards.[55] Even if there is information about a system in the public domain, many ordinary people will lack the expertise required to understand it, and the resources to engage an expert on their behalf. And some automated systems are just inherently complex: they can perform tasks in ways that are quite unfamiliar to humans and thus inscrutable even to experts. These reasons may be more or less compelling in a particular case. But as with any other form of secret government decision making, the resulting opacity is often troubling. It denies people the opportunity to properly understand the government decisions that affect their lives.[56] It makes it more difficult for them to challenge such decisions and enforce their rights. And this, in turn, hinders the courts' ability to develop and clarify the law regulating automated decision making for the benefit of government and the general public.[57]

The ETS cases provide a stark example of these problems. ETS withheld information from the Home Office and the students accused of cheating. ETS refused to disclose its voice recognition system to the Home Office, let alone the students, on the basis of commercial confidentiality. For at least two years, ETS also refused to provide students with the voice recordings used to conclude that they had cheated.[58] In one 2016 decision, the Upper Tribunal described this opacity as 'mildly astonishing'.[59]

ETS also did not have important information about the broader social and technical context for its voice recognition analysis.[60] We touched on some of these important information gaps: the lack of information about the pilot, the lack of information about the TOEIC recordings, the lack of audit trails, the lack of any identifying link between a particular recording and a particular person. The documentation on how the TOEIC had actually been administered at test centres, and thus how the inputs for the voice recognition analysis had been obtained and handled, was incomplete, unclear, and undated. The test centre computers that had been used to make the recordings were unavailable. This limited the capacity for even technical experts to meaningfully scrutinize the ETS evidence.[61]

This opacity flowed through to the Home Office's communications with the students. Its generic decision letters often simply stated that ETS's 'voice verification software' had provided 'significant evidence to conclude that your [TOEIC] certificate was fraudulently obtained by the use of a proxy test taker', and that action was being taken against them accordingly.[62] In 2017, the Upper Tribunal condemned such letters in strong terms:

> They are of extremely poor quality. They obfuscate rather than illuminate. They fail to attach basic, key documents which would have provided necessary explanations and clarification. ... They lacked the standards of care, professionalism and attention demanded in a context entailing draconian consequences for the person alleged to have engaged in deception.[63]

This lack of information undermined people's ability to understand and contest the Home Office's action against them.[64]

In at least some cases, the Home Office's enforcement action was strikingly unfair and heavy-handed. For some students, their first notice of the allegations against them was when a team of Home Office officials arrived at their home and arrested them. They were given no prior notice of the Home Office's proposed decision, nor any opportunity to be heard in relation to it, let alone the evidence supporting it. In February 2015, for example, Abdul, a 30-year-old Bangladeshi man, woke at 6 am to find a team of officials in his bedroom:

> I woke up and found they were in my room. ... I had no idea why they were there. They said: 'You have no legal right to live in this country because you cheated on your English test. ... We accuse you of having had somebody else take the test for you. So we need to deport you'. It was something shocking. We never expected, we never thought, that such a thing could happen. My wife didn't know what to do.[65]

Abdul was arrested and held in immigration detention for 13 days, before being released with reporting conditions.[66]

Advocacy groups and journalists have reported numerous similar stories.[67]

Redress on the fly

Errors and mistakes are an inherent feature of any government decision making system. Even where government does its best to make the right decisions, it invariably goes wrong in some cases. Automated decision making is no different in this respect. In designing and deploying automated systems, therefore, government must consider not only how it should go about making decisions, but also what mechanisms should be in place to provide redress to people when those decisions go wrong. One mechanism for redress is political accountability: drawing public attention to a problematic system; building political pressure on the government to change the system or provide redress for people affected. But the limitations of political accountability, particularly for marginalized groups who may find it difficult to build and wield political power, are well established. All government decision making must be accompanied by redress mechanisms through which an individual can challenge a decision that has adversely affected them, and get an appropriate remedy. This raises a range of important questions for government. What grievances are likely to arise from this decision-making system? What redress mechanisms exist for people to raise those grievances? Are those mechanisms accessible to people in practice? Are they capable of providing people with an effective remedy?

At almost every stage of the ETS saga, the Home Office failed to take basic steps to avoid poor, unfair or unlawful decisions: scrutinizing the accuracy and reliability of the ETS evidence; considering all of the circumstances in each specific case, including other corroborative or contradictory evidence; giving people the substance of this evidence and allowing them an opportunity to be heard before taking action against them. Instead, the Home Office placed the onus of rectifying mistakes on the students and the UK's courts and tribunals. When asked in 2019 about the risk that innocent people had been wrongly accused of cheating, Sir Philip Rutnam affirmed this view: 'the right remedy for people in relation to this is their ability to challenge the decision made by the Department. In this respect, the courts, which are overseeing the system, have played a critical role'.[68] But were these redress systems effective?

In the ETS cases, students who wanted to challenge the Home Office's decisions had two main options for redress. The first was a tribunal appeal, where an independent tribunal judge could examine whether the Home Office had reached the correct decision in their case on the merits: in other words, whether they had actually cheated on their TOEIC. The second mechanism was judicial review, where a judge could examine whether the Home Office's decision complied with basic public law principles, such as the requirements that a decision be rational and procedurally fair. The ETS cases have generated a vast number of challenges in these two channels: over 14,000 cases so far, with more continuing to be brought and heard.[69] From one perspective, this may seem like a sign of a healthy system, with a relatively high number of affected individuals challenging decisions. However, the scandal raises serious questions about whether these redress systems were suited to the job.

Many students found it difficult to access redress for the Home Office's decisions against them, due to a range of legal and practical barriers. The scheme for tribunal appeals was complicated and the Home Office exercised a range of powers to take action against people on the ground of suspected TOEIC fraud. These powers often attracted different appeal rights. In other words, whether a student was entitled to a tribunal appeal, and what kind of appeal, depended on which power the Home Office had exercised in their specific case. This made it difficult for people to work out which redress mechanisms were available to them. It created arbitrary distinctions between different students: some students had more favourable appeal rights than others, based on the powers that had been used to cancel or invalidate their respective rights to remain.[70] It also led to satellite litigation, as students, lawyers, and judges tried to work out which appeal rights applied in a particular case.[71]

While many students had a right to a tribunal appeal, they could generally only exercise it once they had left the UK.[72] This is known as an out-of-country appeal. From the government's perspective, out-of-country appeals are attractive because they facilitate speedy removals, rather than allowing people to remain in the UK while they pursue their challenge. But out-of-country appeals seriously disadvantage the appellants themselves.[73] It can be very difficult and costly to access video conferencing technology outside the UK. The technology can obstruct presentation of the appeal: the appellant is forced to present their case to the judge, navigate bundles of documents, and give evidence via a video connection, with all of the attendant risks of delays and technological failures. And even if the appellant is successful, they are likely to have already suffered serious harm from being forced to leave the UK: relocation costs, loss of employment, disconnection from family, and so on.[74] For many students, therefore, an out-of-country appeal provided no meaningful opportunity for redress.

Students who brought challenges also had to navigate the complex and shifting interaction between these different redress mechanisms. For example, access to judicial review is regulated by a mix of legislation and common law principles. One such principle is that judicial review is a remedy of last resort: if a person has another way of challenging the decision, such as a tribunal appeal, the courts will generally require that they exhaust that remedy before seeking judicial review.[75] In the ETS cases, the courts initially held that an out-of-country appeal was an adequate alternative remedy, despite its serious defects.[76] This had several consequences. It effectively barred many students from accessing judicial review, confining them to an out-of-country appeal with all of its limitations. It also generated significant additional complexity and costs. Many students applied for judicial review – because they were unaware of this broad common law principle, or uncertain about how it might apply in this specific context – only to have their applications summarily refused.[77]

In 2017, however, the courts reversed this position. In the case of *Kiarie and Byndloss*, the Supreme Court recognized that out-of-country appeals would not provide adequate redress in certain cases, especially those where the appellant had to give oral evidence.[78] The Court of Appeal then applied this reasoning to the ETS cases, holding that an out-of-country appeal was not an adequate alternative remedy to judicial review.[79] Judicial review was suddenly available to students caught up in the ETS debacle, but only for those who had managed to maintain their life in the UK through years of uncertainty and insecurity. At the same time, the government made broader legislative changes which further limited access to redress. The Immigration Act 2014 abolished tribunal appeals for most immigration matters, other than human rights claims, with effect from April 2015. This further complicated the legal landscape, because it meant that students had different redress mechanisms available to them depending on when the Home Office had made its decision. It also meant that students affected by decisions made after this time were not entitled to a tribunal appeal, either within or outside the UK. Their only meaningful option for redress was judicial review.

These changes had the overall effect of channelling the ETS cases away from tribunal appeals and toward judicial review. At the same time, however, the courts, the government and many of the students agreed that these cases were best handled by the tribunal system, for reasons we consider further in this chapter. This forced the government to devise a makeshift solution. In short, students were encouraged to make a fresh human rights claim for leave to remain. When this claim was rejected, they would be entitled to an in-country appeal to the tribunal, in which the Home Office would encourage the tribunal to make findings about the original allegation of cheating. If the tribunal found in the student's favour, the Home Office would rescind its original decision and give the student a reasonable opportunity to seek further leave to remain in the UK.[80]

That a redress process was essentially manufactured on the fly is telling. It underscores how the courts and tribunals system was, from the outset, ill-equipped to handle the ETS cases. It also highlights a basic failure of coordination on the government's behalf: legislating to remove appeal rights in 2014, and then having to jerry-rig them back in 2017 and 2018. And in the meantime, students were left to navigate what was, in the words of the Court of Appeal, a 'very messy and unsatisfactory state of affairs'.[81]

Alongside all of the legal complexity, accessing these redress mechanisms was costly.[82] Many students had to spend thousands of pounds to challenge the Home Office's decisions: getting legal advice on their rights under this complex legal framework; making applications that were dismissed on jurisdictional grounds or without a determination on the merits; making fresh applications following the various changes in the legal landscape. For many students, this financial burden was exacerbated by the government's 'hostile environment' policy which, together with the very Home Office decision they were trying to challenge, prohibited them from working, studying, and renting accommodation. The public purse also took a significant hit in having to fund the system managing and responding to these cases.

Many students also faced significant delays in obtaining redress.[83] The Upper Tribunal's decision in the case of *Islam* illustrates this problem.[84] The appellant was a Bangladeshi man who had entered the UK on a student visa in 2010. In November 2014, the Home Secretary decided to remove him from the UK on the ground of TOEIC fraud. The appellant applied for judicial review of this decision, but his application was rejected in January 2016 because he had an out-of-country right of appeal. He then lodged an asylum claim which was refused, and two appeals from that decision were also unsuccessful. In February 2018, the appellant applied to have his judicial review reinstated.[85] The parties then agreed that his case should go through the workaround discussed, which resulted, finally, in a finding by the Upper Tribunal in September 2020 that, in view of all the evidence, the appellant had not cheated on his test. It took almost six years for the appellant to get a conclusive review of the Home Secretary's decision against him.

The limited promise of redress

Students had to navigate a complex, shifting and costly legal landscape, often over a period of multiple years, to get into a position to have a court or tribunal examine their case. Were the courts and tribunals able to resolve the issues presented to them? The ETS cases provide important insights into the effectiveness of different mechanisms of redress for automated decision making. Three issues proved particularly vexing: standard of review; evidence; and remedies.

Judicial review and tribunal appeals have different standards of review. In a judicial review, the judge is confined to reviewing whether the decision under challenge complied with basic public law principles, such as the requirements that a decision be rational and procedurally fair. In a tribunal appeal, the judge applies a much more demanding level of scrutiny. They must determine, in light of all the circumstances, whether the government made the correct decision on the merits.

The ETS cases show the limitations of existing public law principles as a constraint on automated decision making.[86] Numerous students argued that the Home Office had violated these principles by relying on the ETS evidence and by failing to treat them fairly, given the panoply of mistakes and oversights. These challenges were generally unsuccessful, despite a clearly flawed system. In the case of *Mohibullah*, for example, the applicant argued that the Home Secretary's finding that he had engaged in TOEIC fraud was irrational, because of the manifest problems with the ETS testing.[87] The Upper Tribunal rejected this challenge. While the information provided by ETS was 'far from abundant', the Tribunal found that the Home Secretary's decision 'lay within the spectrum of rational decisions open to the hypothetical reasonable decision maker'.[88] In the case of *Islam*, the claimant contended that the Home Secretary had denied him procedural fairness because she had not disclosed the evidence said to support the finding that he had cheated.[89] The High Court rejected this argument. It said that there was 'nothing about the context or circumstances of the present case that would give rise to a duty to disclose documents or witness statements'.[90] The claimant understood the 'gist' of the Home Secretary's decision and 'was able to say what he wanted to say and did so'.[91]

In tribunal appeals, by contrast, students could fully ventilate the problems with the ETS testing and the tribunal could meaningfully scrutinize findings that they had engaged in TOEIC fraud. In the case of *Brar*, for example, the Upper Tribunal concluded, on appeal, that the appellant had not cheated on her test. She had given credible evidence about the circumstances in which she had sat the test.[92] Around the time of sitting the TOEIC, she had passed another language test which showed she had a competent grasp of English, and she had subsequently completed a university degree in English.[93] Meanwhile, it was difficult to have any confidence in the Home Secretary's evidence, given the various flaws discussed.[94] Thousands of students have successfully challenged the Home Office's decisions in this way. From April 2014 to March 2019, the First-tier Tribunal heard 9,277 appeals from people matched to invalid or questionable TOEIC results, of which 40 per cent were successful.[95] According to a Home Office analysis in September 2016, people generally won their appeals either because the tribunal was not persuaded by the ETS testing that the person had cheated, or because the person succeeded in positively demonstrating their innocence.[96]

The ETS cases show that even seriously flawed automated decision making can withstand judicial review on the basis of existing public law principles, which were developed to regulate official decision making by humans. There are multiple lessons that may be drawn from this. One lesson is that it is important to have a range of redress mechanisms that apply different standards of review, including those that can independently assess the merits of automated decisions. The minimum standards imposed by public law are unlikely to comprehend all of the harms that can be caused by bad government automation, at least without significant evolution. Another important lesson is that, as automation grows in government systems, there will likely be growing calls for judges to adapt public law principles to enable meaningful scrutiny of automated decision making on judicial review. There are already signs of this in procedural review of automated decision making. In a series of cases, the courts have required the government to disclose its automated systems where necessary to ensure transparency, fairness, and intelligibility in government decision making.[97] Set against this line of cases, the reasoning in cases such as *Islam* seems meek. The courts have been more cautious about substantive review of automated decision making. As in the ETS cases, the courts are generally slow to conclude that the outputs of technical or scientific systems are so wrong as to be irrational.[98] But there might be room for incremental development here, too. In several recent decisions, the courts have held that automated systems for the calculation of welfare benefits were irrational, because of their unjustified and serious adverse effects on people.[99] In the ETS cases, the Home Office chose to use an automated system that would necessarily result in some number of students being falsely accused. The Home Office failed to take even basic steps to assess or mitigate this risk, or decide whether it was acceptable, for years after the system was deployed. These failures are particularly stark when set against the approach of tribunal judges on appeal, who have consistently emphasized the need to carefully consider all of the relevant circumstances before making a finding of TOEIC fraud. In the future, this kind of recklessness might plausibly be amenable to review on public law principles.[100]

The second issue with the effectiveness of redress was that the ETS cases often involved large amounts of contested evidence.[101] The parties generally adduced conflicting expert evidence about the ETS testing and its potential flaws. Students often provided detailed evidence about the circumstances in which they had sat their tests, to rebut the government's claims of fraud. The conventional view is that judicial review is ill-equipped to resolve factual disputes.[102] The usual procedure is that evidence is given on paper rather than orally, and factual disputes are resolved in favour of the defendant.[103] This view was reflected in the ETS cases. In the case of *Gazi*, a judicial review, McCloskey J held that the evidentiary issues meant that a tribunal appeal was a 'demonstrably superior mechanism for this species of challenge than an application for judicial review'.[104] The applicant's case involved a detailed examination of the Home Office's evidence, including the technical details of ETS's voice recognition analysis.[105] In a judicial review context, there was no opportunity for the judge 'to prove and elucidate these matters via the questioning of witnesses'.[106]

By contrast, in the case of *SM and Qadir*, a tribunal appeal, the students and the key witnesses all gave oral evidence and were subject to cross-examination. The Upper Tribunal's finding in favour of the students turned, critically, on its assessment of their credibility and its concerns about 'the multiple frailties and shortcomings' in the Home Secretary's evidence.[107] The Tribunal concluded that, given the importance of evidence in this context, 'judicial review is an entirely unsatisfactory litigation vehicle for determination of disputes of this kind'.[108] The Court of Appeal echoed these concerns as part of the rationale for the convoluted procedure to funnel the ETS cases into the tribunal appeals system.[109]

The ETS cases show the significance of evidence, and particularly expert evidence, in challenges to automated decisions. The forums in which those challenges are heard must be equipped to receive and scrutinize that evidence. The ETS cases suggest that judicial review is not so equipped. Lord Sales, a Justice of the Supreme Court, in the course of a public lecture, has recently echoed that view, noting that in these proceedings 'the court will have to be educated by means of expert evidence, which on current adversarial models means experts on each side with live evidence tested by cross-examination. This will be expensive and time consuming, in ways which feel alien in a judicial review context'.[110]

But a more optimistic assessment is also possible. First, judicial review has the capacity to receive evidence and resolve contested issues of fact. Contrary to the views expressed in some of the ETS cases, evidence already plays an integral role in many judicial review proceedings.[111] The Administrative Court has an inherent power to direct oral evidence and cross-examination,[112] and the Civil Procedure Rules allow for expert evidence 'which is reasonably required to resolve the proceedings'.[113] Second, if judicial review is to play an effective role in regulating automated decision making, judges must become more willing to apply principles to these systems. Judicial review has a proven capacity to adapt to ensure meaningful scrutiny of government decision making.[114] Without further legislative protections, the growth of automated decision making in government will inevitably demand it does so again.

More generally, the ETS cases highlight some of the difficulties of putting evidence about automated decision making before courts and tribunals. The first difficulty is providing a clear picture of an automated system, when the state of the evidence is evolving over time. When the first cases began to be brought in mid-2014, the Home Secretary relied solely on evidence from two non-expert Home Office officials, who simply described ETS's methodology in general terms. Over the next two years, both sides sought out and adduced more detailed expert evidence on, first, the operation of the voice recognition system itself and, second, the data integrity and security issues with ETS's operations. Finally, in mid-2019, three public inquiries published detailed reports on the ETS cases and the Home Office's decision making: the National Audit Office, the All-Party Parliamentary Group on TOEIC, and the House of Commons Public Accounts Committee.[115] At each of these stages, some questions about the ETS evidence have been answered while other fresh issues have been raised. This has made it very difficult for courts, tribunals, and litigants to develop a settled view on the reliability of the ETS evidence.

In 2016, the Court of Appeal decided several test cases about the weight to be accorded to the ETS evidence, in an attempt to provide some guidance to lower courts and tribunals.[116] But the issues remain contested: in several recent decisions, the Upper Tribunal has concluded that, in light of fresh issues raised in 2019, no weight at all can now be placed on the ETS evidence.[117] Effective redress for automated decision making depends on government and the courts working together to promptly establish a clear and comprehensive picture of the system in question. The ETS cases illustrate both the importance and the difficulty of this task.

There is also a serious potential difficulty in conveying the technical details of an automated system to judges who are not technical experts. In the early cases, where the evidence about ETS's analysis was sparse, judges still often confidently relied on it.[118] In its 2015 decision in the case of *Aziz*, for example, the Upper Tribunal analysed the ETS evidence in the following terms:

[T]he Secretary of State is plainly entitled to rely upon the evidence provided out [sic] her from ETS, which is the world's largest private non-profit educational testing and assessment organization. … It appears to be robust, with not only voice biometric technology being deployed but also an independent check by two analysts, one of whom is experienced, working separately. She is not obliged to provide the names of the centres concerned, nor the details of the equipment used, nor the qualifications of the analysts concerned.[119]

This analysis wholly failed to identify and engage with the potential limitations of ETS's analysis: the accuracy of its voice recognition system, the integrity and security of its data, and so on. To the extent that judges are unfamiliar with automated systems, they will be reliant on the parties and, in particular, those bringing the challenge, to point out its limitations. In more recent cases where there has been extensive evidence about ETS's analysis, judges have nevertheless continued to reach starkly different views on its weight. Two recent decisions from the Upper Tribunal illustrate this point. In the case of *Halima and Ashiquer*, the Tribunal found, allowing the appeal, that the ETS evidence had been 'wholly undermined' by the findings of the 2019 public inquiries.[120] Yet in the case of *Adhikari*, the Tribunal held, dismissing the appeal, that the ETS evidence on the high rate of invalid results was 'overwhelming'.[121] These decisions illustrate the challenges facing judges in synthesizing large amounts of complex and conflicting technical evidence.

The final issue with the effectiveness of redress in the ETS cases was the remedies: what the courts and tribunals could actually do for people wrongly accused of fraud. The ETS cases show how tribunal appeals can provide an effective remedy in individual cases. A successful tribunal appeal provided the appellant with a formal finding that they did not cheat on their test, thus going some way to restore their reputation, and a reasonable opportunity to make further applications to remain in the UK, which would then be determined on their merits.[122] But tribunal appeals have been less effective in addressing the systemic problems with the Home Office's decision making. Most successful appeals have only provided a remedy to the particular person who brought the case. This is a slow and burdensome way to provide redress to the tens of thousands of people affected by the Home Office's decision making. Judicial review has the capacity to provide systemic redress for unlawful automated decision making, as the court can articulate legal limits that apply beyond the particular case before it.[123] But judicial review failed to find much purchase on the Home Office's decision making in the ETS cases. In any case, the ETS cases also highlight the inherent limitations of *ex post facto* remedies: remedies that are only available once a poor or unlawful decision has been made. Many students had already suffered significant harm by the time they got a positive outcome from the tribunal. This all underscores the need for government to ensure that its automated systems are accurate and suitable before deploying them in the first place, whatever redress systems are put in place.

THREE

The Brexit Prototype

Richard Bertinet is a chef who has lived in the UK since 1988.[1] He runs a well-known and popular cookery school in Bath and has penned several award-winning recipe books. A significant portion of the UK's population is made up of people like Richard – people who migrated from EU Member States and made the UK their home. There is still no exact, official count of how many EU citizens are resident in the UK by virtue of free movement rights, but we now know it to be more than four million.[2] That group is embedded within communities across all walks of life. Some have been in the UK for decades, while others arrived more recently. Following the leave vote at the June 2016 Brexit referendum, the status of this group quickly became uncertain. Quite apart from negotiating the rules that would apply, there was the immense challenge of how the new rules would be administered fairly and effectively at the speed required by the Brexit process. In response to this challenge, the Home Office adopted a novel process, known as the EU Settlement Scheme, which included a combination of online applications, partially automated decision making, and cross–departmental data-sharing arrangements. For people like Richard, it was, in the words of then Home Secretary Amber Rudd MP, meant to be 'as easy as setting up an online account at LK Bennett'.[3] Many applications were processed quickly and successfully. But some people, including Richard Bertinet, hit problems and were initially refused indefinite leave to remain in the UK (or 'settled status'). This chapter explores the Home

Office's design of the scheme and its implications for people who need to rely on it.[4]

Negotiating the rules

While far from the only cause of the result, public concerns about levels of immigration were a key driver in the Brexit referendum outcome.[5] Brexit provided an opportunity for the government to change the immigration system in relation to EU nationals, and the removal of free movement rights became a key plank of the UK's Brexit policy. As proclaimed in the preamble to the key piece of legislation establishing the post-Brexit immigration system, the Immigration and Social Security Co-ordination Bill, the central policy objective is to '[e]nd rights to free movement of persons under retained EU law and to repeal other retained EU law relating to immigration'.[6] At the same time, many of the more than four million EU citizens resident in the UK became anxious about their immigration status.

The obvious and pressing need for certainty and clarity on the immigration status of these EU citizens – and UK citizens resident in the EU – is why citizens' rights were considered a priority for both the UK and the EU when negotiations under Article 50 of the Treaty on European Union first started.[7] The first substantive policy document published by the UK government after the referendum sought to set out its intentions on the position of EU nationals living in the UK and British nationals living in other EU Member States.[8] Similarly, a European Commission position paper transmitted to the UK in 2017 emphasized 'the essential principles on citizens' rights' and the importance of securing 'the same level of protection as set out in Union law at the date of withdrawal of EU27 citizens in the UK and of UK nationals in EU27'.[9]

Initial signals of good intent were crystallized in the earliest version of then Prime Minister Theresa May MP's Draft Withdrawal Agreement between the UK and the EU, published in March 2018. In that early draft of the Agreement, the chapter dealing with citizens' rights was one of the areas marked out as being 'agreed at negotiator level and only ... subject to technical revision'.[10] This included an obligation for EU Member States (then including the UK) to 'allow' applications for a residence status that would maintain the rights enjoyed by EU citizens across the Union during a transition period.[11] This discretion found expression in both the first Withdrawal Agreement and the final Withdrawal Agreement.[12] The EU Settlement Scheme is the government system established to realize this commitment.

To make the rules that formed the basis for the EU Settlement Scheme, the government decided to add new rules to the existing Immigration Rules.[13] This was unsurprising. Changing the Immigration Rules has been the preferred mode of implementing changes to immigration policy for successive governments since the Immigration Act 1971 came into force.[14] It also made sense within the government's policy framework: non-European immigration had long been regulated under the Immigration Rules, and using the same approach for the scheme could be understood as part of bringing European migration matters under the general framework of UK immigration law. Nevertheless, using the Immigration Rules as the legal basis for settled status remained controversial. At least three objections are possible. First, the rules do not provide for adequate scrutiny, either when they are made or when they are amended.[15] The rules are drafted by the Home Office and the default position is that they are scrutinized by parliament under the negative resolution procedure – a process about which there have been longstanding concerns and that is generally perceived to be weak.[16] The rules lack the status and authority of primary legislation. It is arguable that the use of the rules is unsatisfactory, given that the scheme implements a commitment in an international treaty and using the rules leaves the scheme open to easy, quick, and repeated changes by Home Office ministers.

What do the rules actually say? Appendix EU of the Immigration Rules makes provision for two immigration statuses. It essentially provides for special forms of indefinite leave to remain and limited leave to remain in the UK.[17] Both the eligibility and suitability criteria under the EU Settlement Scheme are generous when contrasted with the more stringent requirements that apply to permanent residence under the free movement framework and leave to remain under UK immigration law generally.[18] The government has been at pains to emphasize that 'the main requirement for eligibility under the settlement scheme will be continuous residence in the UK'.[19] This is because the eligibility criteria for both types of leave granted under the scheme omit the onerous non-residence-related requirements under free movement rules. For example, Appendix EU has no requirement for applicants to have comprehensive sickness insurance. Applications to the scheme are also subject to less onerous suitability criteria compared to applications for leave in other parts of the Immigration Rules.[20]

Generally, to be eligible for permanent leave to remain in the UK (or 'settled status'), an EU citizen, or their qualifying family member, ought to have completed a continuous period of five years of residence in the UK, with the qualification that 'no supervening event has occurred'.[21] For the purposes of the scheme, a continuous period of residence means an applicant has been resident in the UK, and has not been absent from the country for more than six months within any 12-month period. Furthermore, within that five years, the applicant ought not to have been absent from the UK for a period exceeding 12 months without an 'important reason' justifying their absence. Applicants who lack the requisite five-year period of continuous residence in the UK at the date of application are eligible for a type of limited leave to remain – known as 'pre-settled status'. At a minimum, in order to be granted pre-settled status under the scheme, an applicant ought to evidence at least one month of residence in the UK within the six-month period before they make their application.[22] This will lead to a grant of limited leave to remain in the UK for five years. Even though the EU Settlement Scheme can result in someone being provided with either settled status or pre-settled status, there is an important interplay between the two statuses; applicants granted limited leave to remain under pre-settled status will become eligible for settled status after completing the requisite five-year period of continuous residence in the UK.

Though the substance of the rules underpinning the scheme is not our focus, it does shape the role of the automated system in at least two important ways. First, the thrust of the rules and policy is to make positive grant decisions. This is not typical of decision making in the immigration context and the effects of the same automated system may be very different if deployed in a context with more restrictive rules and policy. Second, the scheme somewhat blurs the traditional distinction between positive and negative decisions. Both settled and pre-settled status decisions are technically positive. However, in many cases, a perceived 'negative' decision is more likely to be a grant of pre-settled status that ought to have been a grant of settled status, as opposed to an outright refusal. There is a significant difference in the rights and entitlements flowing from pre-settled and settled status. Individuals granted pre-settled status are also vulnerable to future changes in the Immigration Rules. Ultimately, this means that we must look beyond any general 'grant' rate to assess how well the automated system is working.

A final noteworthy component of the scheme is that it was essentially created as a 'pop-up' measure, intended not as a permanent fixture, but to facilitate a transition to a 'unified' immigration system in which EU citizens are subject to the same legal framework as other migrants to the UK. The consequence is that there is an important timing dimension to the scheme's structure. The scheme operates on the basis of a 'specified date' by which EU citizens ought to have been resident in the UK in order to be eligible to apply, and a cut-off date by which they must have applied to the scheme (30 June 2021). For a period, these time frames were also contingent on whether a withdrawal agreement was in place.[23] The way the timeframes for the scheme have been conceived can be seen as serving the purpose of incentivizing a steady – and thus manageable – flow of applications to the scheme.[24] However, there was concern that the timeframes might create complexity and confusion for those making applications to the scheme, and potentially for the Home Office too. Furthermore, the time limits may produce harsh results, especially in those cases on the boundary or with otherwise exceptional circumstances. Deadline day hit in June 2021 and many anticipate problems will begin to emerge in the weeks and months to come. Now that the deadline has passed, the challenge shifts to the handling of out-of-time applicants, who are without lawful status in the UK and are likely to be thrown into the hostile environment.

Automate to accelerate

Administering the EU Settlement Scheme placed a significant and complex demand on Home Office officials. The department's job in this respect, as the House of Commons Home Affairs Select Committee observed, was 'unprecedented in scale'.[25] Due to the considerable number of people eligible to apply for settled status over a relatively short, prescribed period, there were inevitably questions about the capacity of administration to cope with the sheer volume of applications, alongside all of its existing workload.

The main response of the Home Office to this challenge was to develop a new 'streamlined' process for applications which relied on two digital platforms: an app downloadable on a mobile phone or tablet, and an online form to be filled in on the government's website.[26] Applicants to the scheme had to submit information on both of these platforms, to satisfy the three broad requirements under the Immigration

Rules: identity, residence, and suitability. Applicants were then directed to an online form to complete. At this point, a National Insurance number was entered, which allowed the Home Office to conduct an automated data check – using existing HM Revenue & Customs (HMRC) and Department for Work & Pensions (DWP) data – to determine the residence element of the scheme's eligibility criteria. Generally, the immigration status granted under the scheme is in the form of an official electronic document accessible through credentials sent via email, not a paper document. The resulting proof of status can only be accessed and shared online.[27]

This process was a significant departure from the traditional Home Office approach to processing and deciding applications. The norm is a paper application on a form, with attached evidence, submitted to a human caseworker, who then makes a decision based on law and policy. A decision letter usually then follows. This typical system was part of the process under the scheme, but it was effectively an ancillary process, with automated data checks given priority in the vast majority of cases.

The automated part of the application process used an algorithm to check HMRC and DWP data for proof of residency.[28] Specifically, three fields of data – an applicant's name, date of birth, and National Insurance number – were sent automatically to DWP and HMRC. Once this information had been received by those two departments, it was transferred to a 'Citizen Matching Layer', which identified the applicant and searched the respective departmental databases for details about the matched applicant. The information was then relayed back to the Home Office and transferred to its 'business logic' – a rule-based algorithm which is yet to be fully disclosed publicly – which processed the information to establish the period of continuous residence in the UK. The basic details of this data-sharing arrangement are set out in Table 3.1. Once an automated check is complete, a caseworker and the applicant saw one of three outcomes: a pass (a five-year

Table 3.1: General data-sharing structure

	HMRC	DWP
Data fields shared	• Employer name • Employer reference • Employer address • Start date • Leaving date • Taxable payment • Payment frequency • Date self-assessment ('SA') record set up • SA employment income • SA self-employment income • SA total income • Tax year • Tax return date of receipt	• Correlation ID • Start date • End date • Benefit type • Date of death • Gone abroad flag • State Pension and New State Pension • Housing Benefit • Jobseekers Employment Support Allowance • Carer's Allowance • Universal Credit • Personal Independent Payment • Disability Living Allowance • Income Support • Maternity Allowance • Incapacity Benefit • Attendance Allowance • Severe Disablement Allowance

period of residence); a partial pass (less than five years of residence); or a fail (meaning the information sent from the Home Office's application programming interface matched no existing records). It was at this final stage of the automated check where human official engagement began. Where the data checks resulted in a partial pass and the applicant was seeking indefinite leave to remain, they were required to submit additional evidence for those periods not sourced by the automated data checks. Officials from the Home Office then dealt with the claim.

Quicker, cheaper, and riskier

The potential benefits of the Home Office's evolved design for determining applications are multiple, but two are often cited as being most important. First, there is the anticipated cost saving. Millions of applications have been effectively determined by automated decisions alone. The Memorandum of Understanding (Process) between HMRC (Data Directorate) and the Home Office is one of two agreements that enables the automated process. It states that the 'estimated API development and delivery charges in respect of Income Verification and EU Exit Settlement Schemes are estimated @ £1.1m'. This figure does not represent all of the costs of the automated aspects of the scheme, but it is indicative that the planned costs will be very low compared to more traditional forms of decision making.[29] This potentially reduces the costs to the taxpayer of administration. However, this claimed benefit ought to come with the caveat that automation does not necessarily eliminate labour and time costs, but could also transfer burdens of the legal and policy framework away from frontline officials (e.g. to the applicants themselves, who become essentially data-entry clerks, and to technologists designing and maintaining the system).[30] The permissiveness of the underlying rules also likely contributes substantially to any cost savings that do materialize – rules that create fewer difficult cases are easier to administer.

Second, the automated checks are very quick, allowing for a high volume of applicants to be processed in a relatively short window of time. Many who passed through them received a decision in a very short time. This is no minor gain: one of the key preferences of citizens using government processes is widely understood to be speed of decision making.[31] By the deadline of 30 June 2021, more than five million applications had been processed by the Home Office.[32] This is a significant achievement. It is also an achievement that is, no doubt, in part the result of the use of automation by the department.

Does this make the EU Settlement Scheme an automation success story? Such a conclusion would be premature. Though it is important to keep the potential benefits of the Home Office's approach to automation in mind, it is equally important to examine carefully what types of problems and grievances it is liable to produce, and thus what shape the demand for redress may take. When thinking about the scope for, and nature of, grievances potentially arising from the scheme, it is helpful to think in terms of two spheres of decision making: the automated decision and the traditional process. In practice, these spheres are closely linked, and the relationship between the two spheres itself raises questions about interactions between officials and technology, but they constitute distinct processes and therefore are liable to create different grievances.[33] There are at least six types of grievance liable to arise in relation to the settled status system.

First, there are those decisions perceived to be wrong or unreasonable. There is a range of familiar concerns in this respect (e.g. decisions that are legally flawed, decisions involving discrimination, refusal to accept liability, and decisions where relevant evidence was not considered). One major concern with the scheme is those cases where applicants simply may not have the necessary evidence, raising a question of how human decision makers will respond to this. The use of automated checks also opens up the possibility of new decision-making behaviours, and thus creates scope for new types of grievance of this kind. One example may be automation bias (i.e. that a decision maker may favour information produced by a computer over the evidence and claims submitted by the applicant through traditional channels).[34] The system of automated checks itself is also liable to produce various problems. For instance, it may be difficult for people to understand or challenge decisions under the scheme. The basic logic of the automated checks is unclear, and it is understood that the checks will not be retained by the Home Office, creating further concerns about the lack of an audit trail. It is unclear whether applicants will be able to know what information about them has been disclosed to the Home Office by DWP and HMRC via automated checks.[35] The automatic check mechanism may also give rise to grievances based on perceived discrimination, which is a widespread concern about algorithmic processes.[36] There is no magic to automated systems: they run on information held in databases. The quality of the decision turns heavily on the quality of the data being fed into the algorithm and the selection of the scope of the databases to be included. Two issues arose in this respect. One is that DWP data are of lesser quality than HMRC data, as HMRC is a digitally advanced public body. The concern here is that vulnerable people are more likely to pass through DWP systems than through HMRC systems (given the functions of each of those departments) and will therefore be at greater risk of being tripped up by DWP's allegedly lower-quality input data. The second is that data from working tax credit, child tax credit, and child benefit records, all managed by HMRC, are not being shared as part of the process. As it is more likely that women are in receipt of these benefits, the exclusion of these data may mean women are at a greater risk of failing the automated check. It is very difficult to examine discriminatory impacts in this context, as the Home Office – despite using digital systems – appears to be collecting and publishing only very limited information on decision making, which excludes basic information such as gender.[37]

Second, there are those grievances that may flow from administrative errors or unacceptable behaviour by staff. Again, many of the grievances liable to arise under the scheme are familiar concerns (e.g. where staff are rude and unhelpful, where staff are incompetent or unreliable, where there is a presumption of deception by staff, where staff do not acknowledge a mistake or offer an apology, where records are lost or misplaced, or where there is no record of information received). Typical risks here may be mitigated by the particular purpose of the scheme, which is designed to be generous. The new automated checks system, however, adds a new layer of complexity, creating the scope for grievances where technical faults afflict individual decisions or where decisions are based on erroneous or otherwise deficient databases. The mainstream use of automation also opens up the risk of mistaken data leaks and similar problems. Furthermore, fixing some problems with the application of technology is not within the gift of the Home Office. For instance, during the second phase of testing, it was found that one EU Member State had not implemented an international biometric data standard in its passports, which caused the app to identify applications as fraudulent.[38] Another Member State had used defective chips.[39]

Third, grievances may arise from what are perceived to be unacceptable delays. The Home Office has a long history of complaints around delay. There is a clear risk, given the scale of the administrative challenge, that caseworkers in the Home Office will be overwhelmed, especially without adequate investment in staffing.[40] By the deadline in 2021, there was an application backlog of more than 500,000 people.[41] With the automated checks, delays may be created by technical errors, the system being overwhelmed, or general all-out system failures. During the second phase of testing, there were two occasions where 'a technical disruption' prevented HMRC data being returned to applicants, one of which resulted in the service being temporarily suspended. Inspectors were told this was 'an unplanned outage of HMRC systems over a weekend', which had resulted in applicants receiving a 'not found' message.[42] Given that speed is one of the widely claimed benefits of automation, a key issue will be whether the underpinning technology and the surrounding human bureaucracy are sufficiently robust to realize that benefit. Many applicants will also be required to provide further documentary evidence to support their applications, which may increase application times.

Fourth, grievances may arise from information or communication failings. Grievances of this sort may arise where people are unaware of the scheme – a widespread concern, particularly in relation to vulnerable groups. They may also relate to a lack of information or awareness about how the system works, such as lack of knowledge about important deadlines.[43] Given the cross-departmental decision-making structure, there may also be data communication issues between different departments. Beyond this, there may be familiar issues of flawed communication of decisions and with decision makers. Perhaps the most important issue in this context, from a legal perspective, is the meaningful communication of a reasoned decision.[44] As the basic logic of the automated checks is not known, it is not entirely clear how the traditional notion of a reasoned administrative decision fits with the scheme. Once a decision is communicated, status will be granted in digital form only. This potentially stores up different types of future communication problems around the already vexed and complex issue of the need to prove status, especially where applications have been made on behalf of others (e.g. children in care).[45]

Fifth, there are grievances that flow from a service being perceived to be unavailable, deficient, or expensive. The particular aspects of the scheme that may pose problems in this respect include, for example, absence of gateway data needed to use services. A clear example of this is a child. Children are unlikely to receive positive results from the data checks because they will not have a National Insurance number and are less likely to engage with DWP or HMRC. The digital dimensions of the scheme also create some particular issues, such as the risk of people being digitally excluded from the service.[46] Another prominent concern around the scheme's use of technology is that parts of the application were only compatible with Android smartphones, cutting out vast parts of the population who do not use Android devices or who do not have a smartphone at all – effectively a form of digital bureaucratic disentitlement.[47]

Finally, there is scope for general objections to the policy underpinning the scheme. In many ways, it is difficult to separate out the policy debate around the scheme from wider policy and political debates surrounding migration and Brexit. For instance, some perceive that the need to apply is wrong in principle. However, there is a range of more specific policy-oriented grievances that could arise under the scheme. The automated data checks add a new set of considerations here too. We are already seeing growing general objections to government departments sharing administrative data and automating processes.[48] Other objections may pertain to the overall lack of transparency in the process.

While the possible benefits of the government's approach must be kept in mind, it is clear that there is a range of risks involved in the automated elements of the EU Settlement Scheme, which are liable to give rise to grievances. Many of these risks are inherent in administrative processes generally, but some are specific to the automated process adopted in the scheme. While caution ought to be shown in judging government innovation at the outset, there is a real sense that the EU Settlement Scheme is a giant experiment in automation, and the full results will not be clear for some time yet as those who may have fallen through the gaps may take some time to emerge. Given the risks involved in the approach taken by the Home Office, a central question is the availability of redress under the scheme, and the extent to which it adequately provides safeguards for individuals.

No deal, no appeal

An applicant refused status under the EU Settlement Scheme before the deadline can make a further application.[49] This means that, in some instances, fresh applications can be made to avoid an onward challenge, potentially providing a quicker and cheaper fix. In this context, redress processes are therefore particularly valuable for those who keep running into a problem which no number of fresh applications can resolve, or those who have been assigned what they believe to be an incorrect status.

Given the factual complexity of some of the cases being processed by the scheme, it was widely thought that a tribunal appeal system would be preferable. When the long-awaited Immigration and Social Security Co-ordination (EU Withdrawal) Bill finally arrived before parliament in late 2018,[50] it was expected that a tribunal appeal right would be included for those making use of the scheme.[51] However, that right was not present in what was a rather thin piece of legislation. As the Home Office indicated in its Statement of Intent on the scheme published in June 2018, primary legislation is required to make provision for a tribunal right, and it was expected that this would be in place when the scheme opened in March 2019.[52] Instead, only a system of administrative review against decisions made under the scheme had been established.[53]

Administrative review is a mechanism whereby another official in the Home Office reviews the papers from the initial decision for errors. The decision can then be changed if there is an error. In recent years, tribunal appeal rights have been restricted across many parts of the immigration system, placing greater emphasis on administrative review.[54] Many applicants, who once had the opportunity of a tribunal appeal before an independent judge, before falling back on judicial review, now only have access to administrative review. There have been some benefits of de-judicialization, such as reduced costs for the state and quicker decisions. However, the growing use of administrative review and the corresponding marginalization of tribunals has resulted in a system where individuals are significantly less likely to succeed in overturning an adverse immigration decision.[55]

Appendix EU of the Immigration Rules identifies two broad categories of decisions amenable to administrative review.[56] First, applicants can seek a review of a decision taken under the scheme if it relates to a refusal on the basis that the applicant does not meet the eligibility requirements. Second, applicants can make an application for administrative review of decisions that relate to the grant of limited leave to remain under paragraph EU3 of Appendix EU. Notably, administrative review is not available against a decision where an application is refused on suitability grounds.[57] In contrast to the administrative review systems generally run by the Home Office, the system under the scheme allows an individual to submit further evidence, which will then be considered alongside their original application by another Home Office caseworker. The central question, however, quickly became whether a full right to a tribunal appeal would eventually appear.

The availability of an appeal right for the scheme was agreed to in the first Withdrawal Agreement. The relevant part of that Withdrawal Agreement provides that the pre-existing safeguards for decisions made under the free movement framework also apply to decisions concerning the residence rights of persons who fall under the scope of the scheme.[58] These safeguards principally include 'the right to access to judicial and, where appropriate, administrative redress procedures in the host Member State to appeal against or seek review of any decision'. Furthermore, under the applicable EU law incorporated into the Agreement, 'the redress procedures shall allow for an examination of the legality of the decision, as well as of the facts and circumstances on which the [decision] is based'. This commitment is partly why the UK government initially promised that a right of appeal against decisions made under the scheme would be introduced. In the government's own words, 'this would allow the UK courts to examine the decision to refuse status under the scheme and the facts or circumstances on which the decision was based'.[59] Even though the Home Office had committed to fully implementing the EU Settlement Scheme in the event of the UK withdrawing from the EU without a withdrawal agreement in place, it was clear that, in that situation, the scheme would lack the appeal right repeatedly promised in previous policy documents.[60] According to a policy paper published by the Department for Exiting the European Union in December 2018, in such circumstances 'EU citizens would have the right to challenge a refusal of UK immigration status under the EU Settlement Scheme by way of administrative review and judicial review'.[61]

This all sounds complex, but the reality was simple: if there was a withdrawal agreement between the UK and EU, then applicants to the scheme would have access to a tribunal appeal. If there was no deal, however, applicants would have no right to a tribunal appeal. Put simply, the government's approach to redress under the scheme was 'no deal, no appeal'.

Ultimately, the UK and the EU reached a withdrawal agreement. The first published version of the Withdrawal Agreement Bill gave ministers the power to make regulations providing for appeal rights against immigration decisions made under the scheme.[62] There was, however, no obligation for the minister to make such regulations. Both provisions were enacted in the European Union (Withdrawal Agreement) Act 2020.[63] A tribunal appeal right eventually materialized by way of The Immigration (Citizens' Rights Appeals) (EU Exit) Regulations 2020, long after the scheme began receiving and determining applications.[64]

It appears that redress was, once again, an afterthought for the Home Office compared to initial application processes. But what is most striking is the Home Office's apparently conscious policy position that the type – and thus quality – of redress would depend on a withdrawal agreement being approved by parliament. The politics of Brexit negotiations was the primary driver of the type of redress system made available to people, not considerations about what kind of redress would be most suitable or effective, particularly given the altered dynamics resulting from automation. The central question is whether the redress system design ultimately adopted for the scheme is the correct one to deal with the grievances liable to arise. Much of this is yet to be seen, but it is already clear that the approach to redress under the scheme does not rest on anything close to a thoughtful understanding of what administrative justice requires in this particular context.

FOUR

Category Errors

Robtel Neajai Pailey is a Liberian academic, activist, and author, currently based at the London School of Economics and Political Science.[1] Since 2006, she has applied for and obtained a range of visas for the UK, including as a tourist, a student, and a skilled worker. Pailey made several of her applications from the US, where she is a permanent resident. The application process was costly and a bit intrusive, but on the whole she felt the experience was 'relatively smooth'. When Pailey applied for a visa from Ghana in 2018, however, she bore significant additional costs and delay. Between the Home Office, the British High Commission in Ghana, and the local visa application centre, no one seemed to know the status of her application or the location of her passport. The delay forced her to cancel a different trip at substantial personal cost, and her request for a refund of the application fees was refused. She described the experience as, simply, 'the absolute worst'.

The true reason for these divergent experiences is and will remain mysterious, but for Pailey, the implication was clear:

> Had I not previously applied from the US, or had enough experiences applying for visas for other countries, I would have been tricked into thinking that the ill-treatment I received was normal. After hearing similar stories from other African colleagues and friends, I remain convinced that the poor service I received was racially motivated and had everything to do with the continent from which I was applying.[2]

One possible explanation for Pailey's experiences is an automated system known as the 'Streaming Tool'. The Home Office deployed the tool in 2015 to help process the millions of visa applications it receives every year. In 2019, however, the tool began to attract public criticism over its opacity and potentially discriminatory operation. This culminated in August 2020, when the Home Office suspended use of the Streaming Tool in the face of a looming legal challenge. This chapter explores how automation was deployed in visa applications and how it ultimately failed.

Visa risks

One of the basic objectives of immigration law and policy is to facilitate the entry of people whose presence in a country is seen as desirable, and to prevent the entry of those seen as undesirable.[3] In the UK, the Immigration Act 1971 provides that most people are not permitted to enter unless they are granted leave to do so.[4] But the details of this system – who is permitted to enter and under what circumstances – are left to the Immigration Rules, which are drafted by the Home Office and set out 'the practice to be followed' by officials in regulating entry under the Act.[5]

The Immigration Rules identify the types of people whose presence in the UK is seen as desirable. They establish a range of different categories of leave – work, study, family, business, visitor, and so on – and eligibility requirements for each category. But from the government's perspective, this leaves open how to identify people who do not fall into these categories, and prevent their entry. It is neither practicable nor desirable to scrutinize every potential entrant in the same way. Every year, tens of millions of people seek to travel to the UK to work, study, visit, or settle.[6] Uniform scrutiny would be highly resource-intensive and inefficient, because the same amount of resources would be spent on someone who is clearly eligible to enter and someone who might not be.

For these reasons, the UK, like other countries, has increasingly adopted, in at least some respects, a risk-based approach to immigration controls.[7] It facilitates the entry of people whose presence is seen as desirable, while targeting controls at people who are taken to pose a risk of breaching immigration law or policy: those who fall outside the recognized categories of leave, and those who might overstay, seek asylum, or otherwise undermine immigration controls or the 'public good' once in the country.[8]

A core element of the UK's risk-based approach is entry clearance. The Immigration Rules allow some nationalities to get leave to enter on their arrival in the UK. For example, a US citizen who wants to visit the UK for a few months can simply fly into Heathrow and swipe their passport at an ePassport gate, which will automatically grant them leave to enter as a visitor for six months.[9] In many cases, however, people must get leave to enter before travelling to the UK. This is known as entry clearance.[10]

The entry clearance process has three main steps.[11] First, the person completes an online form and submits their biometric data and supporting documents to a visa application centre in their country of origin.[12] Second, the application is sent to one of the Home Office's decision-making centres, where an entry clearance officer decides whether the person meets the criteria for the relevant visa.[13] Finally, the person receives the outcome of their application – either a physical visa affixed to their passport or a refusal notice – via the relevant visa application centre.[14]

Entry clearance has a long history in the UK.[15] As far back as 1917, 'aliens' had to get a visa from a British consul before leaving for the UK. Beginning in the 1960s, a growing number of countries were brought under the regime. A key driver of this extension was the government's perception that certain nationalities posed a risk to immigration controls. In 1985, for example, the government imposed entry clearance requirements on Sri Lanka – the first Commonwealth country to be brought under this regime – in an express attempt to stem the arrival of Tamil asylum seekers.[16] Entry clearance is currently required in two circumstances: where a person is coming to the UK for more than six months, or where a person is from one of around 100 countries listed in the Immigration Rules.[17] The vast majority of the listed countries are from the Global South.[18] Without entry clearance, a person is generally unable to enter, or even board their transportation to, the UK.

Entry clearance is a targeted projection of immigration controls beyond the UK's territorial boundaries. As the Home Office put it in 2007, the purpose of entry clearance is 'to target our visa regimes more effectively in order to minimise harm to the UK while allowing nationals of those countries that do not present significant risk to travel to the UK with less scrutiny'.[19]

The risk-based approach to immigration control finds expression in another element of entry clearance decision making: individual risk profiling. Entry clearance sorts nationalities by risk, but profiling purports to sort individuals by risk. Some people are taken to pose a greater immigration risk, on the basis of their personal characteristics, and therefore entry clearance officers subject them to heightened scrutiny before deciding whether to grant them a visa.[20]

Risk profiling has been a feature of UK immigration controls for decades. In 1979, *The Guardian* newspaper revealed that immigration officials were conducting invasive examinations – known colloquially as 'virginity tests' – on Indian, Bangladeshi, and Pakistani women seeking to come to the UK to marry, in an attempt to determine whether they were eligible for leave to enter. This practice was based on racial and sexual stereotypes about women of a particular age, nationality, and circumstances.[21] The revelations prompted the Commission for Racial Equality to conduct a formal investigation into immigration control procedures. In the course of the investigation, the Home Office openly acknowledged that it treated certain people with greater suspicion 'by virtue of their origins and the economic, social or political conditions thought to prevail in their countries'.[22] It justified this approach on pragmatic grounds: people in certain circumstances were more likely to evade immigration controls and thus warranted more scrutiny.[23]

The Commission found that the Home Office's approach was flawed.[24] The Home Office only had statistics for people who had been detected breaching immigration law or policy. These figures provided no reliable guide to the actual rates of breach by different nationalities. And they were influenced by the very approach in question. For example, the high refusal rates for certain groups were generated, at least in part, by the targeted scrutiny applied to them. In practice, the Home Office's approach mostly turned on 'unproven and untested assumptions' about people from 'poor countries' and 'the economic incentives they were thought to have to evade the controls'.[25] This had a disproportionate adverse impact on people of colour:

> The [Home Office's approach] relates essentially to poor countries and brings under particular suspicion visitors from countries which have established ethnic minority communities here. While some such people undeniably evade the controls, so, undeniably – and probably more easily – do considerable numbers of people from wealthier countries who might not be regarded as having strong incentives to do so. The effect of the argument is to cause the procedures to discriminate, in effect, against black people in particular.[26]

The Commission found that members of these groups faced closer examination of their applications, long delays in processing, higher rates of refusal, and less favourable conditions for those granted leave to enter.[27]

Over the next 30 years, risk profiling remained a core part of the Home Office approach. In 2004, the National Audit Office found that practices varied significantly between different entry clearance posts.[28] It noted that:

> To date, few posts have undertaken dedicated research on the nature and extent of the risks in their country and staff understanding of the risks is based largely on experience. There are informal mechanisms for sharing this experience but there have been few attempts to collect and expound knowledge in a systematic manner.[29]

Risk profiling was a largely manual process. Officials at a particular post used 'intelligence' on trends in immigration breaches – for example, figures on people who had been refused entry at ports or made asylum claims after entering the UK – to construct their own profiles of applicants who might pose an immigration risk.[30] These profiles were based on nationality, personal, domestic and employment circumstances, supporting documents, and travel history.[31] Entry clearance officers then manually checked applications against these profiles, and conducted additional checks – for example, contacting the applicant's employer or sponsor – where they found a match between the two.[32]

This approach had clear shortcomings. Risk profiles were often based on limited or outdated data.[33] Some of the profiles included factors that did not seem to be correlated with immigration breaches in practice,[34] while others were too general to be of use in particular cases.[35] And it was inconvenient for officers to have to remember or manually refer to the profiles when considering each application.[36]

In 2015, the Home Office began exploring how to automate the profiling of entry clearance applications.[37] It was thought that automation would help address some of these persistent problems.[38] It would enable the Home Office to collect and analyse large amounts of data, thus providing more reliable assessments of the risks posed by prospective migrants. It could be deployed consistently across the vast and increasing number of visa applications, without relying on the individual diligence or memory of immigration officials.[39] And it would allow the Home Office to assess those applications more quickly and efficiently, thereby reducing costs.[40] The resulting system became known as the 'Streaming Tool'.

Red, amber, green

The Streaming Tool was a computer program which automatically allocated a visa application one of three risk ratings: low ('green'), medium ('amber'), or high ('red'). It was developed by UK Visas and Immigration, a division of the Home Office responsible for the visa system.[41] The tool allocated these ratings in three different ways.[42] First, the tool determined whether the person belonged to one of the nationalities judged by the Home Office as 'posing the greatest threat to the UK immigration control'.[43] The Home Office identified nationalities as suspect based on statistics or intelligence about immigration breaches, or 'adverse events', involving people of that nationality: for example, overstaying, committing a criminal offence while in the UK, or simply having a visa application refused.[44] If the person belonged to one of these nationalities, the tool would allocate their application a (presumably 'red') rating.

Second, the tool matched the person to one of a set of risk profiles, constructed centrally by the Home Office, based on their nationality, the type of application, and the location they were applying from. Each profile had a 'green', 'amber', or 'red' rating, based on global data on the number of 'adverse events' involving people of that group, in proportion to the overall number of applications of that type, over the preceding 12 months.[45] The tool allocated the application a risk rating corresponding to the relevant risk profile.

Third, local entry clearance posts could add their own profiles, rules, or data to the tool. For example, a local profile might flag a particular occupation, sponsor, or travel history as low risk, based on information gleaned by officials at that post. It is not entirely clear how conflicts between these local elements and the other rules applied by the tool were resolved. Posts had some control over the priority given to different rules within the tool, but it appears that generally the centralized profiles and rules took precedence.

These risk ratings had several important consequences for the decision-making process.[46] They determined the kind of decision maker to whom an application was allocated. 'Green' and 'amber' applications were generally allocated to more junior staff, while 'red' applications were assigned to senior or executive officials.[47]

The risk ratings also affected the kinds of checks, or 'enrichment', to be applied to the application.[48] 'Green' applications were generally only subject to basic checks, such as checks of the Police National Computer and the Warnings Index, a watchlist of people of interest to the Home Office.[49] 'Amber' applications were generally also subject to additional checks: for example, checks of employment details, hotel bookings or banking information, examination of documents for potential forgeries, or a telephone interview. 'Red' applications, meanwhile, could be subject to additional, complex checks: for example, face-to-face interviews, counter-terrorism checks, and DNA testing.

The risk ratings further determined the time expected to be spent on the application. Decision-making centres set 'benchmarks' for the number of decisions expected per day by visa category and risk rating. For example, in the Sheffield decision-making centre, entry clearance officers were expected to process 54.9 'green' applications or 18 'red' applications every day.[50] In other words, officers were expected to process 'green' applications three times as quickly as 'red' applications.

Risk ratings also triggered additional layers of internal review. Before granting a 'red' application, or refusing a 'green' application, an official generally had to get the approval of an entry clearance manager.[51] According to the Home Office, the purpose of this review was to 'involve a "second pair of eyes"' in respect of 'decisions that deviate from the norm'.[52]

The natural consequence of this system was that 'red' applications were subjected to much more scrutiny and refused at a much higher rate than 'green' applications. For example, at the Croydon decision-making centre in 2017, 51.41 per cent of 'red' visitor applications were refused, compared to just 3.64 per cent of 'green' applications.[53] In 2019, those figures were 45 per cent and 0.5 per cent, respectively.[54]

In 2019, the government defended the Streaming Tool as providing 'an objective data-driven approach to the consideration of an application', which delivered 'enhanced decision quality' and 'a globally consistent approach' to visa applications.[55] But beneath the cover of new technology, the Streaming Tool actually had much in common with the Home Office's flawed history of risk profiling. This created serious risks of poor or unlawful decision making.

It is important to underscore the significance of entry clearance decision making. As the National Audit Office noted in 2004, poor decision making in this area can have profound consequences.[56] Millions of people go through the entry clearance system every year. From the perspective of applicants and their family and friends, a delay or refusal can mean that they are denied a job, lose a business opportunity, miss a wedding or a funeral, or lose ties to family overseas, alongside the distress and uncertainty of the process itself. Poor entry clearance decision making has negative consequences for the UK, too. If people are wrongly denied entry clearance, or are discouraged from even applying at all, the UK misses out on the skills, spending, investment, and other important contributions that immigrants make to society. There were at least three significant problems with the Home Office's development and use of the Streaming Tool, which affected decision making: the rules applied by the tool; the interaction between decision makers and the tool; and the lack of public information about the tool and how it worked.

New system, old problems

The first problem was the rules applied by the Streaming Tool in processing applications. The rules were derived from the Home Office's data on 'adverse events' involving particular nationalities or groups. The Home Office said that the tool enabled an 'objective data-driven approach' to visa decision making.[57] But these rules were not derived through some advanced process of machine learning. They were written by Home Office officials. And they reproduced some of the same issues that had dogged the Home Office's previous attempts at risk profiling in this area.

The most obvious issue was that the rules directly discriminated on the basis of race. Applicants from ostensibly risky countries were treated with suspicion, and subjected to longer and more intensive scrutiny, simply by virtue of their nationality. And their applications were significantly more likely to be refused than those from other countries.[58] Much of the debate about the use of automated systems in government focuses on the risk that such systems might inadvertently encode and perpetuate discrimination against protected groups.[59] In this case, however, the discrimination was direct and deliberate.

In racially profiling visa applicants, the Streaming Tool contravened one of our most basic legal norms. To excuse this discrimination, the Home Office relied on an authorization granted under the Equality Act 2010, which permits a minister to authorize the use of racial discrimination in the immigration system.[60] While the authorization may have given the Home Office some legal cover, it left the underlying moral issue unresolved. As Lord Nicholls of the House of Lords noted in a 2004 decision: 'Discrimination is an insidious practice. Discriminatory law undermines the rule of law because it is the antithesis of fairness. It brings the law into disrepute. It breeds resentment. It fosters an inequality of outlook which is demeaning alike to those unfairly benefited and those unfairly prejudiced.'[61]

It might be thought that this discrimination, while regrettable, was justified, because it simply reflected the truth about which groups tend to breach the UK's immigration laws. We scrutinize this empirical claim further below. But even accepting the empirical claim, this response misunderstands the nature of the norm against racial discrimination. As Lady Hale observed in another 2004 House of Lords decision:

> The person [engaging in discrimination] may be acting on belief or assumptions about members of the sex or racial group involved which are often true and which if true would provide a good reason for the less favourable treatment in question. But 'what may be true of a group may not be true of a significant number of individuals within that group'. The object of the legislation is to ensure that each person is treated as an individual and not assumed to be like other members of the group.[62]

The very point of the norm against racial discrimination is that racial stereotypes are harmful and inconsistent with respect for the individual, regardless of their statistical accuracy.

Bad data

The data underpinning these racial stereotypes were also flawed. The premise of the Streaming Tool was that the Home Office's data on 'adverse events' reflected the actual incidence of immigration breaches across the population. But these data are necessarily incomplete. As the government has acknowledged, '[i]t is not possible to accurately quantify the number of immigration offenders in the UK as, by their very nature, those that deliberately evade immigration control to enter and stay in the country illegally are not officially recorded until they come to light and are arrested'.[63]

The Home Office has no precise estimate of even the number of people in the UK without leave to remain, let alone the detailed information about their personal characteristics required for individual profiling.[64] Its data thus reflect only those immigration breaches that it detects through intelligence and enforcement activities. And there are good reasons to suspect that, in relation to the Streaming Tool, these data were skewed in several significant respects.

First, the Home Office is heavily reliant on allegations received from members of the public.[65] There is an obvious risk that particular groups may be overrepresented in those allegations due to overt or unconscious bias. For example, the Independent Chief Inspector of Borders and Immigration noted in 2015 that many allegations about illegal working focus on high street Indian and Chinese restaurants, which is 'limiting in terms of organisational knowledge and the nationalities encountered'.[66]

Second, the Home Office's enforcement activity is determined by its own priorities. The Home Office only acts on a small proportion of the allegations it receives: between February and November 2019, it acted on less than 25 per cent of the intelligence it received.[67] One of the Home Office's priorities is to remove people from the UK. In 2019, the Independent Chief Inspector of Borders and Immigration explained how this priority affected enforcement activity on illegal working:

ICE [Immigration Compliance and Enforcement] officers told inspectors that while they did not have targets for the number of deployments, arrests and removals, the latter were still the overriding priority, and senior managers pressed them to target individuals for whom there was a realistic prospect of removal. In practice, this meant that certain nationalities were more likely to be targeted for working illegally. ...

The figures showed that Bangladeshis, Indians and Pakistanis made up over 50% of all arrests made on illegal working visits. Together with Chinese, 4 nationalities accounted for almost two-thirds (63%) of such arrests. Whatever the logic of this approach from a removals perspective, the inference for other nationalities was that the likelihood of being arrested for working illegally was low and the likelihood of removal was negligible.[68]

These priorities skew the Home Office's data. The data do not reflect the actual incidence of immigration breaches involving particular groups, so much as the ease of removing them.

Third, the Streaming Tool created a pernicious feedback loop. If an automated system makes decisions that affect the data that are fed to it in the future, it will tend to produce a feedback loop. Consider, for example, a predictive policing system. The system makes predictions about where crimes are likely to occur, police attend those neighbourhoods and observe crimes occurring, and the police's observations are then fed back into the system, thus apparently confirming its predictions and making it more likely that the system will send police back to those neighbourhoods in the future. Researchers have shown that these systems can generate 'runaway feedback loops': the system's predictions begin to reflect simply the predictions it has made in the past, rather than the true crime rate.[69]

The Streaming Tool appears to have suffered from this problem. The refusal of a visa application constituted an 'adverse event' for the purposes of determining whether a particular nationality would be targeted for additional scrutiny. But if certain nationalities were subject to additional scrutiny, this would naturally lead to a higher rate of refusals for those groups, thus making it more likely that they would continue to be treated as suspect. The Streaming Tool's outputs and its underlying data were unintentionally linked, with one reinforcing the other in a manner detached from the actual incidence of immigration breaches.

These issues are strikingly similar to those raised by the Commission for Racial Equality more than 30 years ago. Then as now, risks of skewed data and feedback loops undermined the Home Office's attempt to use immigration statistics to target particular nationalities. The persistent appeal of a more 'objective', targeted approach to immigration control is matched by persistent problems with the underlying data.

In January 2020, the Home Office completed an internal data protection impact assessment for the latest version of the Streaming Tool. Data protection law requires a person or public body to complete an impact assessment before they engage in any data processing that might jeopardize people's rights and freedoms.[70] The impact assessment must include, among other things, a general description of the processing, an assessment of the risks to rights and freedoms, and the measures envisaged to address those risks.[71] If used properly, these statements can help public officials systematically identify and manage some of the risks posed by automated government decision making.[72] The Home Office's impact assessment for the Streaming Tool failed to identify or grapple with any of the issues we have identified. It asserted that the tool would ensure an approach to visa applications based on evidence, thereby reducing the role of 'subjective judgement and unconscious bias' in the process, without any reference to risks of skewed data or feedback loops.[73] In answer to the question 'Does the proposal involve profiling operations likely to significantly affect individuals?', the impact assessment simply said, 'No'.[74] The Home Office did not even begin to identify the potential problems with the rules applied by the Streaming Tool, let alone take steps to address them.

The computer says 'no'

The second major problem was how decision makers interacted with the Streaming Tool. The issues with the rules applied by the tool were compounded by the risk of automation bias. Automation bias is the tendency for people to rely uncritically on the outputs of automated systems, rather than meaningfully scrutinizing them or giving appropriate weight to contradictory evidence.[75] If an official wholly defers to a system's outputs, they might fail to appreciate that it has made an error in a particular case, or that it does not incorporate all of the factors that they are required to consider. These failings could have legal consequences: they might render the decision unlawful on administrative law grounds, as an impermissible abdication of the official's discretion,[76] or they might trigger rights to information or review under data protection law.[77]

The Home Office has stated publicly that the tool was 'only used to allocate applications, not to decide them'.[78] As Caroline Nokes MP, then Minister for Immigration, put it in June 2019:

> a decision maker assesses every application against the immigration rules, on its individual merits, and taking into consideration the evidence provided by the applicant. ... Streaming does not determine the decision; it determines only the process that is undertaken before a decision officer assesses the application and the requirements for decision manager assurance.[79]

But several features of the tool created a risk that officials would simply rely on its rating to grant or refuse a visa, rather than making an independent judgment in all of the circumstances.[80] The very fact that the tool used the labels 'red', 'amber' and 'green' may have influenced official decision making. Some public bodies in the UK have deliberately avoided attaching these labels to the outputs of their automated systems, to minimize risks of automation bias.[81] The risk rating also operated, in practice, as an independent factor in the ultimate decision to grant or refuse the visa, rather than simply determining the checks applied to an application. The Home Office's internal guidance from October 2017 stated that 'enrichment activity is designed to help inform decision making by providing the decision making [sic] with additional information against which to make a decision on the balance of probabilities. Whilst it may help to mitigate against the risk, it will not always negate it'.[82] This suggests that, in effect, officials treated the tool as providing a default assessment of the risk posed by an application, which could (but might not) be displaced by the checks. This is supported by observations from the Independent Chief Inspector of Borders and Immigration, who found that officials used the risk rating itself to justify their decisions when challenged on them after the fact.[83] This effect was compounded by several other features of the system: the performance 'benchmarks' meant that officials were expected to process 'green' applications quickly, while treating 'red' applications with caution, and an official could generally only depart from the risk rating, by granting a 'red' application or refusing a 'green' application, with the prior approval of their manager.

The risk of over-reliance on the system was further reinforced by the broader decision-making context. Entry clearance is a high-volume, high-pressure decision-making environment. Officials are under significant pressure to process a large number of applications in a short amount of time.[84] As a consequence, before the deployment of the Streaming Tool, entry clearance officers typically adopted what Robert Thomas has described as 'routine working practices': 'while they are expected to examine each application closely, in practice they are faced with such pressures of work that they have little alternative but to process individuals in terms of routines and patterns that facilitate work tasks'.[85] These pressures have continued following the Streaming Tool's deployment. In a 2017 report on entry clearance decision making in Croydon and Istanbul, the Independent Chief Inspector of Borders and Immigration noted this problem:

> Istanbul stated that, in October to November 2016, the number of family visit applications went up, and decisions increased to an average of 137 per [entry clearance officer] per day. This would mean just over three minutes per

decision in a standard working day, which even for an experienced decision maker would allow little time for careful consideration of the evidence, especially where it involved applications streamed Amber or Red.[86]

More recently, officials reported that they were often praised for processing high numbers of applications, rather than for making the right decisions,[87] and they 'felt forced to make a decision based on whatever information they already had', rather than delaying it to carry out further checks.[88] This environment heightened the risk that officials would simply rely on the tool's output when making a decision, rather than considering all of the relevant facts.[89]

It is difficult to assess the extent to which this risk manifested in practice, but there are clear reports of over-reliance. At the Croydon decision-making centre in 2019, 45 per cent of 'red' visitor applications were refused, compared to just 0.5 per cent of 'green' applications.[90] In the same year, some decision makers told the Independent Chief Inspector of Borders and Immigration that there was 'an over-reliance on the Streaming Tool to identify the risks within an application', although their managers tended to disagree.[91] The Chief Inspector ultimately drew the following conclusions from these figures and observations:

> Inspectors were confident from these interviews and observations, together with data on grant rates, that applications streamed RED were not automatically refused and that, having assessed the application individually and, where necessary, tested the evidence, decision makers were comfortable in recommending a visa be granted. However, given the 'daily expectation' levels and the near 100 per cent grant rates (in Croydon inspectors were told the rate was 99.5 per cent), and a limited capacity for quality assurance, it was less clear that all applications streamed GREEN were being assessed on their individual merits.[92]

Whatever the true position, it appears that the Home Office failed to take adequate steps to identify and address the clear risk of automation bias.[93] In 2017, the Independent Chief Inspector of Borders and Immigration concluded that the assurance regime for the Streaming Tool did not take account of the 'danger' of automation bias.[94] The Home Office's impact assessment simply stated that the tool did not 'involve automated decision making'.[95] The only relevant risk it identified was that the tool 'may be misunderstood and mis-reported by the media ... which may harm the reputation of the department', and that, accordingly, '[c]lear press lines have been drafted to explain that the tool does not make decisions and is not artificial learning'.[96]

Secrecy

The third major problem with the Streaming Tool was its opacity. The Home Office declined to disclose much information about the tool itself. In 2015 and 2017, the Independent Chief Inspector of Borders and Immigration published two reports containing some high-level information about the tool.[97] But the details of how the tool had been developed and deployed remained obscure. In 2020, the Chief Inspector recommended that the Home Office should:

> Including as much detail as possible, publish an explanation of how the Streaming Tool works, avoiding jargon and opaque language, and establish an auditable review and assurance system that covers all three RAG ratings, using the outputs to build stakeholder confidence in the Streaming Tool and the way it is used.[98]

The Home Office refused to disclose any further information, however, arguing that it would help 'unscrupulous parties to actively manipulate the immigration system' and undermine the UK's international relations.[99]

It was also impossible for people to know how the Streaming Tool affected the handling of their particular application. UK Visas and Immigration publishes guidance on suggested supporting documents to accompany visa applications.[100] But applications are routinely rejected because of a failure to provide information not specified in the guidance.[101] Applicants are not given an opportunity to submit further evidence before their application is refused; the Home Office suggests that they simply make another application.[102] In 2019, the All-Party Parliamentary Group on Africa found that 'there was still confusion around what is required for a successful application and that this lack of clarity made the system opaque and unfair while increasing the chances of a rejection'.[103] While this problem predates the Streaming Tool,[104] the tool has, since 2015, formed part of this opaque process.

The tool's opacity ultimately engendered public suspicion. In June 2019, the *Financial Times* newspaper reported that the Home Office was using a 'secretive algorithm' to process visa applications, which 'could be discriminating against some applicants on the basis of nationality and age'.[105] This prompted a parliamentary debate, where MPs raised concerns about the lack of transparency and accountability.[106] In January 2020, the Independent Chief Inspector of Borders and Immigration noted that some stakeholders were 'deeply suspicious of the Streaming Tool, believing that it unfairly discriminates against particular applicants'.[107] As well as generating public concern, the system's opacity made it more difficult to challenge the decisions made with the tool.

Whack-a-mole?

Entry clearance decision making generally raises difficult questions when it comes to providing effective redress. On the one hand, many people understandably want to be able to challenge a negative outcome, such as a delay, an error, or a refusal. The decision-making process itself can be intrusive, because applicants can be required to give the Home Office detailed personal and financial information.[108] And a negative outcome can have significant consequences for a person's personal or professional life, if it means that they miss a significant life event or lose a job opportunity. On the other hand, entry clearance decision making is high-volume and often time-sensitive, which complicates the task of providing effective and accessible redress, at least within a limited budget.[109] And the entry clearance system, by design, makes it difficult for applicants, who are located outside the UK, to access domestic courts and tribunals.[110]

The entry clearance system has two main redress mechanisms: administrative review and judicial review.[111] For a mixture of reasons, these mechanisms did little to enable individuals to raise grievances with the Streaming Tool. Administrative review involves another Home Office official reviewing the papers from the initial decision for errors. It is generally available to unsuccessful applicants for entry clearance, subject to certain exceptions.[112] In practice, however, only a small proportion of people apply for administrative review.[113] Many prefer to simply make another application, which is seen as quicker and more effective.[114] In any case, administrative review is not designed to address the broader issues with the Streaming Tool: it is confined to whether the initial decision was mistaken; it is conducted on the papers; and the applicant has no opportunity to submit further evidence.

Judicial review involves a judge examining whether the initial decision complied with basic public law principles. Judicial review is, in principle, capable of providing redress for certain types of grievances with automated decision making. For many entry clearance applicants, however, there is little incentive to pursue judicial review: it is expensive; it is slow, which is a particular difficulty for those trying to make fixed travel dates; and, like any legal proceeding, it is difficult to conduct from overseas. The opacity around the Streaming Tool reinforced these barriers in this case. It would have made little sense for an individual to expend time and money judicially reviewing the Streaming Tool, when it was unclear how it operated or what impact it had, if any, in their particular case.

The limitations of these redress mechanisms are evidenced by the fact that the Streaming Tool was in operation for almost five years before it was challenged in court. In late October 2019, however, the Joint Council for the Welfare of Immigrants (JCWI), an immigrants' rights group, began the process of seeking judicial review of the tool.[115] JCWI's claim was supported by Foxglove, a new legal and advocacy group focused on justice in technological systems.[116] In early August 2020, soon after JCWI had formally commenced proceedings, the Home Office conceded the claim and shelved the tool, pledging to 'redesign' the visa application process 'with an open mind in considering the concerns you have raised'.[117] There are at least three important points to be taken from this successful litigation.

One lesson from this litigation is that specialist legal and advocacy groups can help overcome some of the barriers to redress in this area. Various commentators have voiced concerns about the limitations of redress mechanisms for automated decision making that are based on individual rights.[118] The effectiveness of these mechanisms depends on an individual having the time, money, knowledge and motivation to bring a challenge.[119] Specialist legal and advocacy groups can avoid some of these constraints.[120] JCWI and Foxglove were much better placed to challenge the Streaming Tool than most individual visa applicants. They understood the intricacies of UK immigration law and policy, including the longstanding issues with entry clearance decision making and data collection that might skew the tool's operation. They had expertise in emerging technologies and the problems they often present when deployed in government decision making. And they were based in London, and thus geographically close to the decision making and the courts. JCWI and Foxglove were also able to help resolve the coordination problem faced by the vast number of individuals potentially subject to the tool. Each of those individuals would have had an interest in the tool being challenged, to ensure that the UK's visa decision making was lawful. But most of them would have had no particular incentive to bring the challenge themselves, given the costs, stress, and time demands of litigation. JCWI and Foxglove could effectively bear these costs on behalf of all of the individuals potentially subject to the tool, thus enabling the issues to be ventilated.

The litigation also shows how judicial review can be used to hold automated decision making to account. Three aspects of judicial review were important in this case. The first was the disclosure. The judicial review procedure requires the parties to a prospective judicial review to communicate before proceedings are issued, to identify and try to resolve the issues in dispute.[121] During this time, the government party is subject to a 'duty of candour': a duty to disclose all matters that are relevant to the issues in the proceedings.[122] This procedure enabled JCWI and Foxglove to get a much better picture of how the Streaming Tool worked and how it affected the handling of applications. In response to requests for information in this pre-action correspondence, the Home Office disclosed a range of internal policy documents, together with written explanations of the Streaming Tool's design and operation.[123] This helped JCWI and Foxglove to identify the risks posed by the tool – for example, the potential for a feedback loop and the prospect that officials would over-rely on the risk rating – with much greater precision. This demonstrates how judicial review can play a role in helping to overcome the opacity of public sector automated systems.

The second important aspect of judicial review in this case was the substantive legal principles. JCWI claimed that the Home Office's use of the Streaming Tool was unlawful on a broad range of grounds, drawing on equality and discrimination law, common law principles of administrative law, and data protection law.[124] This shows how claimants can, and may need to, draw on a range of legal tools, including administrative law, human rights law, equality and discrimination law, and data protection law, to hold automated decision making to account. JCWI's claim also shows how issues with the design or deployment of automated systems can be brought under well-recognized legal categories, for the purpose of litigation. For example, JCWI argued that the Streaming Tool's feedback loop meant that it produced results that were irrational and therefore unlawful. Courts have reviewed government decisions on the ground of irrationality for centuries.[125] This illustrates how longstanding public law principles can be translated to address the new challenges presented by automated decision making.

The third important aspect of judicial review in this case was the remedies. JCWI and Foxglove's challenge was systemic. Their arguments focused on the Streaming Tool in general, rather than its use in particular cases. They sought remedies prohibiting the use of the tool altogether, rather than simply requiring the Home Office to remake an individual decision.[126] In the event, the court was not called on to grant these remedies, because the Home Office conceded the claim and agreed to discontinue its use of the tool. But the litigation demonstrates how judicial review can be used to challenge entire automated systems.

The challenge brought by JCWI and Foxglove also highlights some deep questions about redress for automated decision making. Following its concession, the Home Office agreed to redesign the visa application process. It pledged that the redesign would 'carefully consider and assess' the points raised by JCWI and Foxglove, 'including issues around unconscious bias and the use of nationality, generally, in the Streaming Tool'.[127] It seems inevitable that the Home Office will eventually deploy a new version of the tool. The basic drivers of the move toward automated decision making in this area remain the same: a large and growing number of applications; budgetary constraints; the broader risk-based approach to immigration controls. In this way, the tool was simply the most recent expression of a logic deeply embedded in UK immigration law and policy. At present, the only way to ensure that any new version of the tool avoids the issues we have discussed is continued vigilance from organizations such as JCWI and Foxglove, among others. This is a demanding task. As Margot Kaminski puts it, because automated systems evolve over time, '[t]rying to regulate the quality of these systems through individual challenges will constitute an elaborate game of whack-a-mole'.[128] That task is complicated by the fact that, at the same time, the Home Office is deploying similar systems in many other areas of decision making, including through its 'Digital Services at the Border' programme.[129] Individual, *ex post facto* remedies are important but may ultimately struggle to secure fairness in automated immigration systems.

FIVE

Precautionary Measures

The three systems we have explored in this book barely scratch the surface of automation in government immigration systems. They are systems which have, for various reasons and through various means, come into public view. But automated systems are being developed and deployed in many more corners of the immigration bureaucracy. The current trajectory, both in the UK and around the world, is toward increasingly automated immigration systems.

From the transitional and experimental phase that we are currently in, it is clear that automated immigration systems can bring benefits. For example, automation has allowed millions of people to get their status under the EU Settlement Scheme quicker than would have otherwise been possible, reducing delay and associated anxiety. These systems also seem to have some success in reducing decision-making costs. However, automated systems also pose clear and real risks of failure. These failures can occur, and have already occurred, at both individual and systemic levels, with disastrous effects for individuals and their families, as well as wider society and the economy. The resultant harms must be taken seriously, and certainly more seriously than the Home Office appears to have taken them to this point.

The examples considered in this book show that there is a pattern of risky experimentation with automated systems in the Home Office. This experimentation has five key features. First, the Home Office deploys a novel automated system: an automated system that is used to perform a task previously performed by a person. This decision is made wholly within the Home Office, with little or no prior parliamentary or public debate. Second, the Home Office has several aims in deploying the system. It intends that the system will perform the specific task more efficiently, more consistently, and more accurately than its manual equivalent. But at the same time, the Home Office aims to test whether the system, or something similar, could be used in other areas of the bureaucracy. Governments often view populations on the margins of society – migrants, prisoners, and so on – as a convenient testing ground for new technologies: they are seen to have weaker claims to respect for their rights and interests and, consequently, they are generally left with weaker legal and political safeguards.[1] Third, there is little evidence for the ostensible benefits of the system prior to its deployment. These benefits also tend to accrue to the government or the general, non-migrant population, rather than those subject to the system. Petra Molnar has suggested that, for government, it is often 'a more urgent priority to deport people faster rather than use technological interventions to catch mistakes that are made in improperly refused immigration and refugee applications'.[2] Fourth, the system poses serious risks of harm. Poor or unlawful automation often has significant consequences for those people subject to the system. But with immigration systems, those consequences are especially serious: distress, delay, disruption, detention, and deportation. And when automation goes wrong, it can harm many more people than a comparable manual process, because its key attraction is the capacity to make a large number of decisions quickly and efficiently. The harms from botched automated systems can also extend to the Home Office itself, which risks policy failure, wasted resources, and a loss of public confidence in its operations. Finally, the Home Office fails to take adequate steps to identify or mitigate these risks, or to respond to problems when they arise.

The question that arises, therefore, is how we can better approach developing and deploying automated immigration systems. Building administrative institutions that can apply law and policy efficiently while ensuring fairness for individuals is a constant challenge. The use and integration of new technologies in this setting does nothing to change this fundamental predicament.[3] Striving for good administration is a task riddled with unresolvable tensions. Gunter Teubner argues that almost all legal and political institutions are placed under the competing demands of efficacy, responsiveness, and coherence.[4] That is to say, people demand that administrative bodies be successful in managing their role, responsive to the public will, and aligned with the foundational commitments of society. Teubner contends that any design or redesign of an administrative institution that sought to improve its performance in one of these three respects would almost certainly undermine at least one of the other two. As Jerry Mashaw puts it, 'structuring and controlling administrative institutions' can be seen as a 'perpetually unsatisfactory project of institutional design', which even has 'a certain fatalistic hue'.[5] In other words, 'from one or another perspective, every government institution will fail, or be seen as partially failing'.[6] But this does not mean that, when significant developments such as automation occur, we should shy away from considering how underlying tensions are affected and whether a better balance can be struck overall. We can strive to fail better and to do justice as best we can within the limits of the possible.[7] To that end, we offer here the central lessons that emerge from the Home Office's experiments with automated systems so far. We group these lessons according to the three aspects of automated systems we identified at the outset: the underpinning rules, the decision-making process, and the avenues available for people to seek redress.

In relation to the 'rules' – the law and guidance underpinning a particular system, and how they frame its development and use – the main lesson is one of a failure by omission rather than commission. In the examples we have explored, and other similar systems elsewhere, the rules are generally stated and do not contemplate automation in any detail or at all. Law is typically only a very broad canvas upon which automated systems are sketched.[8] When rules are made, parliamentary and public debate about automation is therefore generally very limited – if there is any debate at all – and serious debate only usually arises when things have gone wrong or are about to do so. Few rules specifically regulate the development of automated systems in the Home Office. Digital designers responsible for building automated systems are quickly occupying the space – and assuming the power – that was traditionally held by 'street-level bureaucrats'.[9] We know little about how these digital designers work in government, how they view the law, and the role that law plays in their approach to designing automated systems.[10] There is much that remains to be uncovered and understood in this area, but as the UN Special Rapporteur on extreme poverty and human rights recently observed, automated systems in the public sector are at risk of becoming a 'law-free zone'.[11] An important implication is that the critical question of whether we should automate systems at all is usually left to government bodies and digital designers, without wider debate. We need legislators, judges, regulators, and government officials to develop appropriate rules for automated decision making.[12] These rules might be specific to a particular use case (e.g. automated facial recognition technology) or a particular sector (e.g. immigration), or cut across a range of technologies and areas of government. The rules might establish substantive limits on automated systems, or suitable procedures for their development and deployment, or some combination of the two. Certain types of rulemaking will be more appropriate than others in particular contexts. For example, while parliament could lay down broad principles to govern automated decision making, it would likely need others to fill in how these principles apply in specific cases. Ultimately, we need to centre law in the design and development of these systems, both within the Home Office and more widely.[13]

In relation to the 'decision making', the starting point is to ask: 'what types of problems is an automated decision-making process liable to give rise to?' These problems must be considered alongside any claims about the benefits that automation will purportedly yield. Michael Adler has devised a general typology of administrative grievances, conceived in relation to non-digital administration, which can assist with identifying the potential problems in this respect (see Table 5.1).[14] Adler's framework disaggregates types of grievance and groups them in 'bottom-up' (i.e. ordinary) and 'top-down' (i.e. elite) terms.[15] This is a helpful typology as it 'meshe[s] well with the ways in which people define and describe the problems that they experience but would probably not have reflected some very important analytical distinctions'.[16] Using Adler's typology as a starting point, it is possible to think through how automation can alter the traditional dynamic of grievances.[17]

Our three case studies show that automation is likely to alter the nature of the grievances arising from government decision making. Consider, for example, a person who believes that they have been wrongly refused a visa because an automated system, similar to the Streaming Tool discussed in Chapter Four, has erroneously identified them as high-risk. In a sense, this person is in the same situation as any other person faced with what seems to be a wrong government decision, whether automated or manual. But automation may alter the nature of this grievance in at least three ways. First, automation may make certain grievances more common. Our case studies suggest that, at present, automated decision making is particularly prone to produce certain grievances: decisions perceived as wrong or unreasonable; decisions involving discrimination; and information or communication problems.

Second, automation may change the underlying causes of the grievance. The visa refusal might be the product of the system's incomplete and skewed data, combined with the decision maker's over-reliance on its outputs. In that

Table 5.1: Typology of administrative grievances

Top-down typologies	Bottom-up typologies	Composite typologies	Examples
Error of fact Error of law Abuse or misuse of discretion/ discrimination	Unjust decisions and actions	Decision wrong or unreasonable	Decision perceived to be wrong or unfair Decisions involving discrimination Decisions that involve imposition of unreasonable conditions Refusal to accept liability
Incompetence Unreliability Lack of respect Lack of privacy Lack of responsibility No apology	Administrative errors Unacceptable treatment by staff	Administrative errors Unacceptable treatment by staff	Records lost or misplaced No record of information received Staff rude and unhelpful Staff incompetent or unreliable Presumption of 'guilt' by staff Threatening or intimidating behaviour by staff Staff do not acknowledge mistake or offer apology
Unacceptable delay	Delay	Unacceptable delays	Delays in making appointments Delays in making decisions Delays in providing services

Top-down typologies	Bottom-up typologies	Composite typologies	Examples
Lack of participation No information	Information or communication problems	Information or communication problems	Lack of information Conflicting or confusing information Poor communication Objections ignored by staff Lack of privacy
Lack of choice Lack of resources No value for money	Service unavailable Service deficient in quality or quantity	Benefit/service unavailable or deficient in quality or quantity or too expensive	Benefit/service withdrawn (either for everyone or some people) Benefit/service deficient in quantity or quality
Policy	General objections to policy	General objections to policy Other grievances	Policy unacceptable Other types of grievance not covered in the composite typologies

case, the government would need to take distinctive steps to avoid grievances of this kind (e.g. establishing practices and procedures to counter automation bias), as compared to similar grievances arising from conventional decision making.

Third, automation may aggravate certain grievances. The very fact that the mistake is made by an automated system, rather than a human being, may affect a person's perception of it. This could be because the very use of an automated system is perceived as 'impersonal and dehumanising'.[18] Or it could be because the automated system, such as the Streaming Tool, is perceived as having reached its decision by simply comparing the person to a range of historical data and 'looking at the statistics', rather than treating them as an individual.[19] Our case studies indicate that the Home Office has, thus far, failed to consider and address the varied ways in which automation may create problems for the people subject to it.

It is therefore unsurprising that similarly little thought has been given to the issue of 'redress' in this area. Elsewhere, there has been a range of attempts to generate principles of good redress design. Legal scholars have, for instance, developed general accounts of the value of legal forms of justice compared to political and other modes of securing justice against the state.[20] The most advanced account of this issue can be found in the work of Varda Bondy and Andrew Le Sueur.[21] They point out, in the context of traditional administrative systems, that we do not have sufficiently developed understanding of what is 'a good "fit" between the types of grievance and the redress mechanism'.[22] The use of automated systems once again illuminates this deficit. Our three case studies show that policy makers and digital designers in the Home Office have repeatedly failed to respond to the changing dynamics created by automation. This has often meant that people cannot access redress mechanisms or, if they can, that such mechanisms do not provide an effective remedy. Without a proactive and creative approach to redress for automated decision making, existing redress systems will continue to fail, and governments will continue to come under pressure to make rushed, costly, and often unfair changes in response to these failures. At present, people who are subject to poor or unlawful automated decisions are often left trying to put square pegs in round holes. The less time, money, and energy they have to spend on this, the better.

In each of these three areas, patterns are still emerging and lessons are still being learned the hard way. That will, no doubt, continue to be the case: automated systems generate many more uncertainties regarding rules, decision making, and redress than traditional decision-making processes. These uncertainties warrant a precautionary approach to the development and use of automated immigration systems. The precautionary principle is an ethical and decision-making principle, which came to prominence in the context of environmental regulation but is increasingly used in various regulatory contexts.[23] As the Court of Appeal put it recently, the 'essence' of the principle is that 'measures should be taken, where there is uncertainty about the existence of risks, without having to wait until the reality and seriousness of those risks becomes fully apparent'.[24] Similarly, the High Court recently observed that 'the State does not have to await the accrual or manifestation of actual harm before acting and it can act to forestall that adverse eventuality. As a matter of logic there is no reason why good government should not involve precautionary measures in a range of different policy fields'.[25] We have highlighted a series of automated immigration systems that have created clear and significant risks and been accompanied by inadequate safeguards.

Our case for a precautionary approach to automated immigration systems is not intended as a counsel of despair. Thought about the state has long been driven by fear of the state's capacity to harm the public.[26] Much contemporary thought on the administrative state is still prone to such tendencies, typically now expressed in terms such as 'risk management'.[27] We should be appropriately sceptical about such framings. So too should we be sceptical about applying the precautionary principle where it is not justified.[28] However, the contemporary use of automated decision making in immigration systems justifies a precautionary approach. As we have shown, the use of these systems essentially amounts to a giant, risky experiment, in which people's lives are staked against often marginal and speculative benefits. There may well be a point in the future where the precautionary principle is redundant in this context: where we have clear evidence that automated immigration systems can be used lawfully and fairly, and so we can focus more on their ability to promote the public interest and less on risks of injustice for individuals. It requires a great deal of faith – too much – to conclude that we are already at that point.

What questions does the precautionary principle require us to ask about automated immigration systems? Any precautionary principle has two basic elements.[29] The first is the threshold: what kinds of harms, and what kinds of evidence, warrant a precautionary approach to an activity? In this context, precaution is warranted because, as our case studies show, automated immigration systems pose credible risks of very serious harm, to potentially very large groups of people. The onus rests on government to rebut this claim, by publishing sufficient evidence on the operation and impact of such systems. Until this is done, we should be cautious about any proposal to deploy a new automated immigration system.

This leads to the second element of the precautionary principle, which is the remedy: what precautionary action should decision makers take in relation to the activity? Different systems will require different responses, but it is possible to sketch some of these precautions in broad terms. There must be clear, public rules establishing appropriate, substantive limits on automated immigration systems. There must be participatory processes for the development and deployment of these systems, involving both independent experts and the communities subject to them. Systems must be developed and deployed incrementally: by analogy to previous, successful examples, rather than by radical, large-scale experiments. Systems must also be subject to appropriate monitoring and auditing, preferably by an independent, expert, and public institution which can run the rule over them. Government must keep the records necessary for this to occur. And there must be public redress processes for individuals affected by these systems, which are both accessible and effective. Ultimately, if the Home Office is to continue to experiment with automated systems, it must take appropriate precautionary measures. This is essential to ensure that society can benefit from government automation without exposing individuals to unacceptable risks.

Notes

Foreword

[1] Committee on Standards in Public Life, *Artificial Intelligence and Public Standards: A Review by the Committee on Standards in Public Life* (February 2020) 6.

one The Home Office Laboratory

[1] Immigration Act 2014 pt 4.

[2] Independent Chief Inspector of Borders and Immigration, *The Implementation of the 2014 'Hostile Environment' Provisions for Tackling Sham Marriage: August to September 2016* (December 2016) [7.4]–[7.16]; Home Office, *Equality Impact Assessment* (30 November 2020).

[3] Home Office, *Equality Impact Assessment* (30 November 2020) 5.

[4] D. Taylor and F. Perraudin, 'Couples face "insulting" checks in sham marriage crackdown' (*The Guardian*, 14 April 2019) <www.theguardian.com/uk-news/2019/apr/14/couples-sham-marriage-crackdown-hostile-environment>.

[5] D. Taylor and F. Perraudin, 'Couples face "insulting" checks in sham marriage crackdown' (*The Guardian*, 14 April 2019) <www.theguardian.com/uk-news/2019/apr/14/couples-sham-marriage-crackdown-hostile-environment>; R. Wright, 'Crackdown on sham marriages leaves migrants in limbo' (*Financial Times*, 10 September 2018) <www.ft.com/content/3a724c10-ac47-11e8-94bd-cba20d67390c>.

[6] See HM Government, *2025 UK Border Strategy* (CP 352, December 2020); National Audit Office, *Digital Services at the Border* (HC 1069, 9 December 2020); House of Commons Public Accounts Committee, *Digital Services at the Border* (HC 936, 12 March 2021); HM Government, *New Plan for Immigration: Legal Migration and Border Control: Strategy Statement* (CP 441, May 2021).

[7] C. Black and C. Safak, *Government Data Systems: The Bureau Investigates* (The Bureau of Investigative Journalism, 2019).

[8] HM Government, *2025 UK Border Strategy* (CP 352, December 2020) 21.

[9] See generally on the complexity of frontline official decision making: M. Lipsky, *Street Level Bureaucracy: Dilemmas of the Individual in Public Services* (Russell Sage, 1980) and B. Zacka, *When the State Meets Street* (Harvard University Press, 2017).

10 M. Williams, 'Legislative Language and Judicial Politics: The Effects of Changing Parliamentary Language on UK Immigration Disputes' (2017) 19 *British Journal of Politics and International Relations* 592.

11 Law Commission, *Simplification of the Immigration Rules: Report* (HC 14, No 338, 2020).

12 There may be numerous reasons for this, including applicants not having access to historic documents or documents from another jurisdiction.

13 J.L. Mashaw, *Bureaucratic Justice: Managing Social Security Disability Claims* (Yale University Press, 1983) (discussing the 'bureaucratic rationality' model).

14 A recent example being the Windrush scandal. See: House of Commons Home Affairs Committee, *The Windrush Generation* (HC 990, 3 July 2018); W. Williams, *Windrush Lessons Learned Review* (HC 93, March 2020).

15 An 'automated system', as we are using that term, involves a computer that can perform actions or make decisions without a human being's direct involvement. The rules applied by the computer might be written by a person, or they might be derived through machine learning, where a separate automated system finds patterns in existing data which are then applied to classify or make predictions about new situations. Automated decisions result from a system that is fully or partially automated.

16 P. Dunleavy, H. Margetts, S. Bastow, and J. Tinkler, *Digital Era Governance: IT Corporations, the State, and e-Government* (Oxford University Press, 2008) 70.

17 See, e.g., Department of Economic and Social Affairs, *UN E-Government Survey 2016* (2016).

18 See generally M. Veale and I. Brass, 'Administration by Algorithm? Public Management Meets Public Sector Machine Learning' in K. Yeung and M. Lodge, *Algorithmic Regulation* (Oxford University Press, 2019).

19 See, e.g., P. Molnar and L. Gill, *Bots at the Gate: A Human Rights Analysis of Automated Decision Making in Canada's Immigration and Refugee System* (The Citizen Lab, 2018); C. Jones, *Automated Suspicion: The EU's New Travel Surveillance Initiatives* (Statewatch, 2020); P. Molnar, *Technological Testing Grounds: Migration Management Experiments and Reflections from the Ground Up* (EDRi and Refugee Law Lab, 2020); *Report of the Special Rapporteur on contemporary forms of racism, racial discrimination, xenophobia and related intolerance* (A/75/590, 10 November 2020).

20 HM Government, *2025 UK Border Strategy* (CP 352, December 2020); National Audit Office, *Digital Services at the Border* (HC 1069, 9 December 2020); House of Commons Public Accounts Committee, *Digital Services at the Border* (HC 936, 12 March 2021); HM Government, *New Plan for Immigration: Legal Migration and Border Control: Strategy Statement* (CP 441, May 2021).

21 E. Jones and C. Safak, 'Can algorithms ever make the grade?' (Ada Lovelace Institute, 18 August 2020) <www.adalovelaceinstitute.org/blog/can-algorithms-ever-make-the-grade/>.

22 S. Coughlan, 'A-levels and GCSEs: Boris Johnson blames "mutant algorithm" for exam fiasco' (*BBC*, 26 August 2020) <www.bbc.co.uk/news/education-53923279>.

23 BBC, 'Chief education civil servant Jonathan Slater sacked after exams row' (*BBC*, 26 August 2020) <www.bbc.co.uk/news/uk-politics-53920146>.

24 L. Dencik, A. Hintz, J. Redden, and H. Warne, *Data Scores as Governance: Investigating Uses of Citizen Scoring in Public Services* (Data Justice Lab, December 2018); C. Black and S. Safak, *Government Data Systems: The Bureau Investigates* (The Bureau of Investigative Journalism, 2019).

25 See C. Black and C. Safak, *Government Data Systems: The Bureau Investigates* (The Bureau of Investigative Journalism, 2019); HM Government, *2025 UK Border Strategy* (CP 352, December 2020); National Audit Office, *Digital Services at the Border* (HC 1069, 9 December 2020); House of Commons Public Accounts Committee, *Digital Services at the Border* (HC 936, 12 March 2021); HM Government, *New Plan for Immigration: Legal Migration and Border Control: Strategy Statement* (CP 441, May 2021).

26 For an introduction to the field of administrative justice, see: J. Tomlinson, R. Thomas, M. Hertogh, and R. Kirkham, *The Oxford Handbook of Administrative Justice* (Oxford University Press, 2021). See also: J. Tomlinson, *Justice in the Digital State: Assessing the Next Revolution in Administrative Justice* (Bristol University Press, 2019).

27 For further elaboration of this framework, see: J. Tomlinson, 'Justice in Automated Administration' (2020) 40(4) *Oxford Journal of Legal Studies* 708.

two Testing Systems

1 A. Gentleman, ' "I never met anyone who cheated": student's anger at English test scandal' (*The Guardian*, 1 May 2019) <www.theguardian.com/uk-news/2019/may/01/some-have-been-disowned-the-students-accused-of-cheating>; House of Commons Public Accounts Committee, *Written evidence submitted by Raja Noman Hussain (ELT0069)* (July 2019) <data.parliament.uk/WrittenEvidence/CommitteeEvidence.svc/EvidenceDocument/Public%20Accounts/English%20language%20tests%20for%20overseas%20students/Written/103603.html>; V. Stacey, 'UK: TOEIC victim receives residence permit' (*The PIE News*, 5 January 2021) <thepienews.com/news/toeic-victim-granted-uk-residence-permit>.

2   House of Commons Public Accounts Committee, *English Language Tests for Overseas Students* (HC 2039, 9 September 2019) 11.

3   See generally A. Blackledge, 'Inventing English as Convenient Fiction: Language Testing Regimes in the United Kingdom', in G. Extra and others (eds), *Language Testing, Migration and Citizenship: Cross-National Perspectives on Integration Regimes* (Continuum, 2009) 87.

4   British Nationality and Status of Aliens Act 1914 s.2(1)(b).

5   See, e.g., House of Commons Home Affairs Committee, *Managing Migration: The Points Based System* (HC 217-I, 15 July 2009) [115]; HC Deb, 9 June 2010, c11WS.

6   See, e.g., The Rt Hon T. May MP, 'Immigration' (Speech to Policy Exchange, 5 November 2010) <www.gov.uk/government/speeches/immigration-home-secretarys-speech-of-5-november-2010>; HC Deb, 22 March 2011, vol 525, cols 855–8.

7   H. Wilkins, A. Pratt, and G. Sturge, *TOEIC Visa Cancellations* (House of Commons Library, CDP 2018/0195, 29 August 2018) 2.

8   National Audit Office, *Investigation into the Response to Cheating in English Language Tests* (HC 2144, 24 May 2019) figures 2 and 9.

9   R. Watson, 'Student visa system fraud exposed in BBC investigation' (*BBC*, 10 February 2014) <www.bbc.co.uk/news/uk-26024375>.

10 HC Deb, 9 June 2010, c11WS; HC Deb, 22 March 2011, vol 525, cols 855–8.

11 See House of Commons Public Accounts Committee, *Oral Evidence: English Language Tests for Overseas Students, HC 2039* (10 July 2019) Q23, Q25, Q64, Q81.

12 House of Commons Public Accounts Committee, *Oral Evidence: English Language Tests for Overseas Students, HC 2039* (10 July 2019) Q81.

13 National Audit Office, *Investigation into the Response to Cheating in English Language Tests* (HC 2144, 24 May 2019) [2.18].

14 See, e.g., Immigration and Asylum Act 1999 s.10(1)(b); Nationality, Immigration and Asylum Act 2002 s.76(2)(a); Immigration Rules paras 321A(2), 321A(5), 322(2), 323(ia). Some of these provisions have since been amended.

15 National Audit Office, *Investigation into the Response to Cheating in English Language Tests* (HC 2144, 24 May 2019) [3.26]; All-Party Parliamentary Group on TOEIC, *Report of the APPG on TOEIC* (18 July 2019) 23–4.

16 National Audit Office, *Investigation into the Response to Cheating in English Language Tests* (HC 2144, 24 May 2019) [3.29].

17 H. Wilkins, A. Pratt, and G. Sturge, *TOEIC Visa Cancellations* (House of Commons Library, CDP 2018/0195, 29 August 2018) 5.

18 *R (Ahsan) v Secretary of State for the Home Department* [2017] EWCA Civ 2009 [1] (Underhill LJ).

19 Treasury Board of Canada, *Directive on Automated Decision-Making* (5 February 2019) <www.tbs-sct.gc.ca/pol/doc-eng.aspx?id=32592>; Commonwealth Ombudsman, *Automated Decision-making: Better Practice Guide* (2019) <www.ombudsman.gov.au/__data/assets/pdf_file/0030/109596/OMB1188-Automated-Decision-Making-Report_Final-A1898885.pdf>.

20 Treasury Board of Canada, *Directive on Automated Decision-Making* (5 February 2019) <www.tbs-sct.gc.ca/pol/doc-eng.aspx?id=32592>; Committee on Standards in Public Life, *Artificial Intelligence and Public Standards: A Review by the Committee on Standards in Public Life* (February 2020) 52.

21 National Audit Office, *Investigation into the Response to Cheating in English Language Tests* (HC 2144, 24 May 2019) [2.18].

22 National Audit Office, *Investigation into the Response to Cheating in English Language Tests* (HC 2144, 24 May 2019) [2.7].

23 *SM and Qadir v Secretary of State for the Home Department* [2016] UKUT 229 [21]–[22] (McCloskey J and Saini DUTJ).

24 *SM and Qadir v Secretary of State for the Home Department* [2016] UKUT 229 [63] (McCloskey J and Saini DUTJ).

25 All-Party Parliamentary Group on TOEIC, *Report of the APPG on TOEIC* (18 July 2019) 21–2.

26 National Audit Office, *Investigation into the Response to Cheating in English Language Tests* (HC 2144, 24 May 2019) [2.7]–[2.10]; House of Commons Public Accounts Committee, *English Language Tests for Overseas Students* (HC 2039, 9 September 2019) [9]; All-Party Parliamentary Group on TOEIC, *Report of the APPG on TOEIC* (18 July 2019) 22.

27 *R (Gazi) v Secretary of State for the Home Department* [2015] UKUT 327 [11] (McCloskey J).

28 P. Harrison, *In the Matter of ETS TOEIC Fraud: Report on Testing of Samples Undertaken by ETS* (J P French Associates, 5 February 2015) 19; P. French, *Report on Forensic Speaker Comparison Tests Undertaken by ETS* (J P French Associates, 20 April 2016) 6–7.

29 P. Harrison, *In the Matter of ETS TOEIC Fraud: Report on Testing of Samples Undertaken by ETS* (J P French Associates, 5 February 2015) 17–20; P. French, *Report on Forensic Speaker Comparison Tests Undertaken by ETS* (J P French Associates, 20 April 2016) 5.

30 P. Harrison, *In the Matter of ETS TOEIC Fraud: Report on Testing of Samples Undertaken by ETS* (J P French Associates, 5 February 2015) 30.

31 P. French, *Report on Forensic Speaker Comparison Tests Undertaken by ETS* (J P French Associates, 20 April 2016) 5.

32 P. French, *Report on Forensic Speaker Comparison Tests Undertaken by ETS* (J P French Associates, 20 April 2016) 12.

[33] See, e.g., House of Commons Public Accounts Committee, *Oral Evidence: English Language Tests for Overseas Students, HC 2039* (10 July 2019) Q96, Q108; *Secretary of State for the Home Department v Alam* [2020] UKAITUR JR131382014 (24 September 2020).

[34] House of Commons Public Accounts Committee, *Oral Evidence: English Language Tests for Overseas Students, HC 2039* (10 July 2019) Q96, Q108.

[35] All-Party Parliamentary Group on TOEIC, *Report of the APPG on TOEIC* (18 July 2019) 22.

[36] Joint Memorandum of Christopher Stanbury, Peter Sommer and Richard Heighway (27 July 2016).

[37] National Audit Office, *Investigation into the Response to Cheating in English Language Tests* (HC 2144, 24 May 2019) [2.20], [3.8]–[3.11].

[38] All-Party Parliamentary Group on TOEIC, *Report of the APPG on TOEIC* (18 July 2019) 14.

[39] See, e.g., *Secretary of State for the Home Department v Upreti* [2018] UKAITUR HU060512016 (5 January 2018).

[40] See, e.g., *Meethal v Secretary of State for the Home Department* [2019] HU103662018 (13 March 2019).

[41] See, e.g., *Secretary of State for the Home Department v Islam* [2020] UKAITUR HU170902019 (28 September 2020).

[42] See, e.g., *Rehman v Secretary of State for the Home Department* [2018] UKAITUR IA000802017 (27 July 2018).

[43] See, e.g., National Audit Office, *Investigation into the Response to Cheating in English Language Tests* (HC 2144, 24 May 2019) [2.22].

[44] National Audit Office, *Investigation into the Response to Cheating in English Language Tests* (HC 2144, 24 May 2019) [2.18].

[45] Sir D. Norgrove, 'Letter to Rt Hon Stephen Timms MP' (9 September 2019) <uksa.statisticsauthority.gov.uk/wp-content/uploads/2019/09/20190909_Letter_to_Stephen_Timms_MP_TOEIC-1.pdf>.

[46] See B. Green and Y. Chen, 'The Principles and Limits of Algorithm-in-the-Loop Decision Making' (2019) 3 *Proceedings of the ACM on Human-Computer Interaction*, https://doi.org/10.1145/3359152, for further discussion of these issues.

[47] *SM and Qadir v Secretary of State for the Home Department* [2016] UKUT 229 [22] (McCloskey J and Saini DUTJ).

[48] National Audit Office, *Investigation into the Response to Cheating in English Language Tests* (HC 2144, 24 May 2019) [2.24].

[49] *SM and Qadir v Secretary of State for the Home Department* [2016] UKUT 229 [63] (McCloskey J and Saini DUTJ).

[50] National Audit Office, *Investigation into the Response to Cheating in English Language Tests* (HC 2144, 24 May 2019) [2.5].

[51] *AB v Secretary of State for the Home Department* [2020] UKAITUR HU115662015 (4 February 2020).

52 House of Commons Public Accounts Committee, *English Language Tests for Overseas Students* (HC2039, 9 September 2019) [2].

53 P. Alston, *Statement on Visit to the United Kingdom* (Special Rapporteur on extreme poverty and human rights, 16 November 2018) <www.ohchr. org/documents/issues/poverty/eom_gb_16nov2018.pdf> ('a major issue with the development of new technologies by the UK government is a lack of transparency'); Committee on Standards in Public Life, *Artificial Intelligence and Public Standards: A Review by the Committee on Standards in Public Life* (February 2020) 6, 17–19 ('Public sector organisations are not sufficiently transparent about their use of AI and it is too difficult to find out where machine learning is currently being used in government'); Centre for Data Ethics and Innovation, *Review into Bias in Algorithmic Decision-Making* (November 2020) 133 ('Currently, it is difficult to find out what algorithmic systems the UK public sector is using and where').

54 J. Burrell, 'How the Machine "Thinks": Understanding Opacity in Machine Learning Algorithms' (2016) *Big Data & Society*, https://doi. org/10.1177/2053951715622512

55 J. Cobbe, M. Seng Ah Lee, H. Janssen, and J. Singh, 'Centering the Law in the Digital State' (2020) 53(10) *Computer* 47.

56 *Osborn v Parole Board* [2013] UKSC 61 [68]–[69] (Lord Reed).

57 *R (UNISON) v Lord Chancellor* [2017] UKSC 51 [69]–[72] (Lord Reed).

58 *SM and Qadir v Secretary of State for the Home Department* [2016] UKUT 229 [22] (McCloskey J and Saini DUTJ); National Audit Office, *Investigation into the Response to Cheating in English Language Tests* (HC 2144, 24 May 2019) [2.21]; All-Party Parliamentary Group on TOEIC, *Report of the APPG on TOEIC* (18 July 2019) 16.

59 *SM and Qadir v Secretary of State for the Home Department* [2016] UKUT 229 [63] (McCloskey J and Saini DUTJ).

60 Joint Memorandum of Christopher Stanbury, Peter Sommer, and Richard Heighway (27 July 2016).

61 In *R (Saha) v Secretary of State for the Home Department* [2017] UKUT 17 [15] (McCloskey J and Rintoul UTJ), the Upper Tribunal noted the experts' 'recurring lament' about 'the quantity and quality of material actually available to us'.

62 See, e.g., *R (Saha) v Secretary of State for the Home Department* [2017] UKUT 17 [15] (McCloskey J and Rintoul UTJ).

63 *R (Saha) v Secretary of State for the Home Department* [2017] UKUT 17 [66] (McCloskey J and Rintoul UTJ).

64 National Union of Students, *The TOEIC Scandal: An Ongoing Injustice* (May 2018) 14; Migrant Voice, *'I want my future back': The international students treated as guilty until proven innocent* (July 2018) 12 ('All the research participants highlighted how the Home Office failed to provide

any evidence of the allegation against them. They could not, therefore, contest the evidence – a basic tenet of any system of justice'.)

65   Migrant Voice, *'I want my future back': The international students treated as guilty until proven innocent* (July 2018) 19–21.

66   Migrant Voice, *'I want my future back': The international students treated as guilty until proven innocent* (July 2018) 19–21.

67   See, e.g., Migrant Voice, *'I want my future back': The international students treated as guilty until proven innocent* (July 2018); A. Gentleman, ' "I never met anyone who cheated': student's anger at English test scandal' (*The Guardian*, 1 May 2019) <www.theguardian.com/uk-news/2019/may/01/some-have-been-disowned-the-students-accused-of-cheating>.

68   House of Commons Public Accounts Committee, *Oral Evidence: English Language Tests for Overseas Students, HC 2039* (10 July 2019) Q97.

69   National Audit Office, *Investigation into the Response to Cheating in English Language Tests* (HC 2144, 24 May 2019) [3.30]–[3.33].

70   For example, a student whose leave to remain was cancelled under para 321A of the Immigration Rules while they were outside the UK had more favourable appeal rights than a student whose leave to remain was invalidated under s.10(1)(b) of the Immigration and Asylum Act 1999 while they were inside the UK.

71   See, e.g., *R (Ali) v Secretary of State for the Home Department* [2014] UKUT 494; *Amin v Secretary of State for the Home Department* [2015] UKAITUR IA260342014 (19 February 2015).

72   See Migrant Voice, *'I want my future back': The international students treated as guilty until proven innocent* (July 2018) 38.

73   See Independent Chief Inspector of Borders and Immigration, *An Inspection of the Non-Suspensive Appeals Process for 'Clearly Unfounded' Asylum and Human Rights Claims: October 2013–February 2014* (July 2014) [7.1]–[7.12]; *R (Mohibullah) v Secretary of State for the Home Department* [2016] UKUT 561 [90] (McCloskey J and Rintoul UTJ); *R (Kiarie) v Secretary of State for the Home Department* [2017] UKSC 42 [66]–[74] (Lord Wilson).

74   J. Tomlinson and B. Karemba, 'Tribunal Justice, Brexit, and Digitalisation: Immigration Appeals in the First-tier Tribunal' (2019) 33 *Journal of Immigration, Asylum and Nationality Law* 47, 57.

75   See, e.g., *R (Glencore Energy UK Ltd) v Revenue and Customs* [2017] EWCA Civ 1716 [51]–[58] (Sales LJ).

76   See, e.g., *R (Mehmood) v Secretary of State for the Home Department* [2015] EWCA Civ 744; *R (Sood) v Secretary of State for the Home Department* [2015] EWCA Civ 831.

77   See Migrant Voice, *'I want my future back': The international students treated as guilty until proven innocent* (July 2018) 38.

78 [2017] UKSC 42.

79 *R (Ahsan) v Secretary of State for the Home Department* [2017] EWCA Civ 2009.

80 This convoluted workaround was endorsed by the Court of Appeal in *Khan v Secretary of State for the Home Department* [2018] EWCA 1684.

81 *R (Ahsan) v Secretary of State for the Home Department* [2017] EWCA Civ 2009 [129] (Underhill LJ).

82 House of Commons Public Accounts Committee, *English Language Tests for Overseas Students* (HC 2039, 9 September 2019) [17]. See generally Migrant Voice, *'I want my future back': The international students treated as guilty until proven innocent* (July 2018).

83 See, e.g., the students profiled in Migrant Voice, *'I want my future back': The international students treated as guilty until proven innocent* (July 2018).

84 *Secretary of State for the Home Department v Islam* [2020] UKAITUR HU170902019 (28 September 2020).

85 This was in light of the decision in *R (Ahsan) v Secretary of State for the Home Department* [2017] EWCA Civ 2009.

86 See J. Cobbe, 'Administrative Law and the Machines of Government: Judicial Review of Automated Public-sector Decision-making' (2019) 39 *Legal Studies* 636.

87 [2016] UKUT 561.

88 *R (Mohibullah) v Secretary of State for the Home Department* [2016] UKUT 561 [63] (McCloskey J and Rintoul UTJ). The same conclusion has been reached in a range of other decisions. See, e.g., *R (Islam) v Secretary of State for the Home Department* [2017] EWHC 3614 [54]–[56] (Michael Fordham QC) ('I am satisfied that the Secretary of State was entitled on the material available to her to reach the conclusion that she did'); *R (Gazi) v Secretary of State for the Home Department* [2015] UKUT 327 [35] (McCloskey J) ('the Respondent's evidence … was sufficient to warrant the assessment that the Applicant's TOEIC had been procured by deception'); *R (Saha) v Secretary of State for the Home Department* [2017] UKUT 17 [68] (McCloskey J and Rintoul UTJ) ('The Secretary of State's decisions have a demonstrably rational basis and readily withstand the species of challenge which the Applicants have elected to mount'); *R (Kaur) v Secretary of State for the Home Department*, Application number JR 8997-15 [47] (Freeman UTJ) ('evidence obtained through the ETS Look-up Tool entitled a reasonable decision-maker to refuse an application made in these circumstances'). The latter decision is reported as an attachment to *R (Nawaz) v Secretary of State for the Home Department* [2017] UKUT 288.

89 *R (Islam) v Secretary of State for the Home Department* [2017] EWHC 3614 [7], [9] (Michael Fordham QC).

90 *R (Islam) v Secretary of State for the Home Department* [2017] EWHC 3614 [12] (Michael Fordham QC).

91 *R (Islam) v Secretary of State for the Home Department* [2017] EWHC 3614 [35] (Michael Fordham QC). See also *R (Mohibullah) v Secretary of State for the Home Department* [2016] UKUT 561 [76]–[84] (McCloskey J and Rintoul UTJ), and the unreported decision of the Upper Tribunal in *Uddin v Secretary of State for the Home Department* (JR/2263/2016, 30th March 2017). Cf. *R (Mir) v Secretary of State for the Home Department* [2020] UKAITUR JR008182016 (13 October 2020) [40]–[43] (Allen UTJ), where the Upper Tribunal found that the Home Secretary's failure to put the allegations of fraud to the applicant was procedurally unfair.

92 *Brar v Secretary of State for the Home Department* [2021] UKAITUR HU110862019 (28 January 2021) [20] (Smith UTJ).

93 *Brar v Secretary of State for the Home Department* [2021] UKAITUR HU110862019 (28 January 2021) [21]–[23] (Smith UTJ).

94 *Brar v Secretary of State for the Home Department* [2021] UKAITUR HU110862019 (28 January 2021) [17] (Smith UTJ).

95 National Audit Office, *Investigation into the Response to Cheating in English Language Tests* (HC 2144, 24 May 2019) [3.30]–[3.37].

96 These cases accounted for almost 75 per cent of the successful appeals analysed by the Home Office. See National Audit Office, *Investigation into the Response to Cheating in English Language Tests* (HC 2144, 24 May 2019) [3.30]–[3.37].

97 See J. Maxwell and J. Tomlinson, 'Government Models, Decision-Making, and the Public Law Presumption of Disclosure' (2021) 25 *Judicial Review* 296.

98 *R (Mott) v Environmental Agency* [2016] EWCA Civ 564 [69]–[82] (Beatson LJ). See also *R (Members of the Committee of Care North East Northumberland) v Northumberland County Council* [2013] EWCA Civ 1740 [34]–[37] (Sullivan LJ); *R (Spurrier) v Secretary of State for Transport* [2019] EWHC 1070 [173]–[175] (Hickinbottom LJ and Holgate J).

99 See, e.g., *Secretary of State for Work and Pensions v Johnson* [2020] EWCA Civ 778.

100 See Lord Sales, 'Algorithms, Artificial Intelligence and the Law' (Sir Henry Brooke Lecture, London, 12 November 2019) <www.supremecourt.uk/docs/speech-191112.pdf>, referring to 'the well-established jurisprudence on challenges to adoption of policies which are unlawful' and 'recent decisions on unfairness challenges to entire administrative systems'.

101 *Majumder v Secretary of State for the Home Department* [2016] EWCA Civ 1167 [27] (Beatson LJ) ('every ETS/TOEIC case will be fact sensitive, with the outcome determined on the basis of the evidence adduced by the parties').

102 See, e.g., *R (A) v Croydon London Borough Council* [2009] UKSC 8 [33] (Lady Hale).

103 See, e.g., *R v Board of Visitors of Hull Prison, ex parte St Germain (No 2)* [1979] 1 WLR 1401, 1410H (Geoffrey Lane LJ).

104 *R (Gazi) v Secretary of State for the Home Department* [2015] UKUT 327 [36] (McCloskey J).

105 *R (Gazi) v Secretary of State for the Home Department* [2015] UKUT 327 [36]–[37] (McCloskey J).

106 *R (Gazi) v Secretary of State for the Home Department* [2015] UKUT 327 [37] (McCloskey J).

107 *SM and Qadir v Secretary of State for the Home Department* [2016] UKUT 229 [100]–[101] (McCloskey J and Saini DUTJ).

108 *SM and Qadir v Secretary of State for the Home Department* [2016] UKUT 229 [102] (McCloskey J and Saini DUTJ).

109 *Ahsan v Secretary of State for the Home Department* [2017] EWCA Civ 2009 [115] (Underhill LJ); *Khan v Secretary of State for the Home Department* [2018] EWCA 1684 [39]–[40] (Singh LJ).

110 Lord Sales, 'Algorithms, Artificial Intelligence and the Law' (Sir Henry Brooke Lecture, London, 12 November 2019) <www.supremecourt.uk/docs/speech-191112.pdf>.

111 See J. Tomlinson, A. Harkens, and K. Sheridan, 'Judicial Review Evidence in the Era of the Digital State' (2020) *Public Law* 740.

112 *R (PG) v London Borough of Ealing* [2002] EWHC 250 [21] (Munby J).

113 CPR 35.1.

114 See, e.g., *R (A) v Croydon London Borough Council* [2009] UKSC 8 [33] (Lady Hale) ('The only remedy available is judicial review and this is not well suited to the determination of disputed questions of fact. This is true but it can be so adapted if the need arises. … That the remedy is judicial review does not dictate the issue for the court to decide or the way in which it should do so').

115 National Audit Office, *Investigation into the Response to Cheating in English Language Tests* (HC 2144, 24 May 2019); All-Party Parliamentary Group on TOEIC, *Report of the APPG on TOEIC* (18 July 2019); House of Commons Public Accounts Committee, *English Language Tests for Overseas Students* (HC 2039, 9 September 2019).

116 *Secretary of State for the Home Department v Shehzad and Chowdhury* [2016] EWCA Civ 615; *Majumder v Secretary of State for the Home Department* [2016] EWCA Civ 1167.

[117] See also *Halima and Ashiquer v Secretary of State for the Home Department* [2020] HU037412019 and HU037462019 (27 April 2020); *Secretary of State for the Home Department v Islam* [2020] HU170902019 (28 September 2020).

[118] See, e.g., *Said v Secretary of State for the Home Department* [2015] UKAITUR IA395862014 (12 May 2015); *Farooq v Secretary of State for the Home Department* [2015] UKAITUR IA389622014 (29 May 2015).

[119] *Secretary of State for the Home Department v Aziz* [2015] UKAITUR IA260032014 (22 May 2015) [32] (Taylor UTJ).

[120] *Halima and Ashiquer v Secretary of State for the Home Department* [2020] HU037412019 and HU037462019 (27 April 2020) [2] (McWilliam UTJ).

[121] *Adhikari v Secretary of State for the Home Department* [2019] UKAITUR HU084142019 (9 December 2019) [29] (Canavan and Keith UTJJ).

[122] See *Khan v Secretary of State for the Home Department* [2018] EWCA 1684; Home Office, *Educational Testing Service (ETS): Casework Instructions* (18 November 2020) 9.

[123] See the discussion of judicial review in Chapter Four.

three The Brexit Prototype

[1] A. Gentleman, 'French chef's struggle to get settled status after 31 years in UK' (*The Guardian,* 30 August 2019) <www.theguardian.com/politics/2019/aug/30/french-chef-richard-bertinet-settled-status-uk>.

[2] Home Office, 'EU Settlement Scheme quarterly statistics, March 2021' (1 June 2021) <www.gov.uk/government/statistics/eu-settlement-scheme-quarterly-statistics-march-2021/eu-settlement-scheme-quarterly-statistics-march-2021>. The initial estimates ranged between 3.5 million and 4 million. See Migration Advisory Committee, *EEA Migration in the UK: Final Report* (2018); M. Sumption and Z. Kone, *Unsettled Status? Which EU Citizens Are at Risk of Failing to Secure their Rights after Brexit?* (The Migration Observatory, 2018).

[3] 'Rudd says online EU registration will be "as easy as shopping at LK Bennett"' (*The Guardian*, 23 April 2018) <www.theguardian.com/politics/2018/apr/23/amber-rudd-online-eu-registration-system-lk-bennett>.

[4] At the time of writing, the application window had just closed and, as we make clear elsewhere, it is still to be seen how the full process develops.

[5] Lord Ashcroft's election day poll of 12,369 voters found that 33 per cent of leave voters said the main reason for their vote was that leaving 'offered the best chance for the UK to regain control over immigration and its own borders'.

[6] Immigration and Social Security Co-ordination (EU Withdrawal) Bill (HC 309).

[7] HM Government, *Rights of EU Citizens in the UK* (June 2017).

[8] HM Government, *The United Kingdom's Exit from the European Union: Safeguarding the Position of EU Citizens Living in the UK and UK Nationals Living in the EU* (Cm 9464, June 2017).

[9] European Commission Task Force for the Preparation and Conduct of the Negotiations with the United Kingdom Under Article 50, *Position Paper on 'Essential Principles on Citizens' Rights'* (TF50 (2017) 1/2 Commission to UK, 12 June 2017).

[10] European Commission, *Draft Agreement on the withdrawal of the United Kingdom of Great Britain and Northern Ireland from the European Union and the European Atomic Energy Community (Version highlighting the progress made in the negotiation round with the UK of 16–19 March 2018)* (2018).

[11] European Commission, *Draft Agreement on the withdrawal of the United Kingdom of Great Britain and Northern Ireland from the European Union and the European Atomic Energy Community (Version highlighting the progress made in the negotiation round with the UK of 16–19 March 2018)* (2018) art. 17(a).

[12] *Agreement on the withdrawal of the United Kingdom of Great Britain and Northern Ireland from the European Union and the European Atomic Energy Community, as endorsed by leaders at a special meeting of the European Council on 25 November 2018* (2018); *Agreement on the withdrawal of the United Kingdom of Great Britain and Northern Ireland from the European Union and the European Atomic Energy Community* (2019/C 384 I/01).

[13] Immigration Rules Appendix EU and Immigration Rules Appendix AR (EU).

[14] For a recent overview of the role of the Immigration Rules, see Law Commission, *Simplification of the Immigration Rules: Report* (HC 14, No. 338, 2020).

[15] Immigration Act 1971 s.3(2).

[16] The negative resolution procedure is a type of parliamentary procedure that applies to statutory instruments. Its name describes the form of scrutiny that the SI receives from parliament. An SI laid under the negative procedure becomes law on the day the minister signs it and automatically remains law unless a motion – or 'prayer' – to reject it is agreed by either House within a certain number of days. There is critical analysis on the use and scrutiny of statutory instruments, which spans the history of the modern administrative state in the UK. See, e.g., R. Fox and J. Blackwell, *Devil Is in the Detail: Parliament and Delegated Legislation* (Hansard Society, 2014); E.C. Page, *Governing by Numbers: Delegated Legislation and Everyday Policy Making* (Hart, 2001). Note, however, there is a debate about whether the rules are strictly delegated legislation. See *Odelola v Secretary of State for the Home Department* [2009] UKHL 25; *R v Chief Immigration Officer, Heathrow Airport* [1976] 1 WLR 979; *R v Secretary of State for Home Affairs* [1977] 1 WLR 766; *R (Munir) v Secretary of State*

for the Home Department [2012] UKSC 32; *R (Alvi) v Secretary of State for the Home Department* [2012] UKSC 33.

17 Though the statuses are popularly referred to as 'settled status' and 'pre-settled status', these two phrases do not appear in the Immigration Rules. Instead, Appendix EU uses the staple immigration language of 'indefinite leave to remain' and 'limited leave to remain'.

18 Home Office, *EU Settlement Scheme: Statement of Intent* (21 June 2018).

19 Home Office, *EU Settlement Scheme: Statement of Intent* (21 June 2018) [2.3].

20 Home Office, *EU Settlement Scheme: Statement of Intent* (21 June 2018) [1.13]. However, see Joint Council for the Welfare of Immigrants, *Broken Promises: The EU Nationals the Government Intends to Remove after Brexit* (25 October 2018).

21 Immigration Rules Appendix EU para EU11.

22 Immigration Rules Appendix EU para EU14.

23 Department for Exiting the European Union, *Citizens' Rights – EU Citizens in the UK and UK Nationals in the EU* (6 December 2018) [7]–[9].

24 S. Altmann, C. Traxler, and P. Weinschenk, 'Deadlines and Cognitive Limitations' (IZA Institute of Labour Economics, Discussion Paper No. 11129, 2017).

25 House of Commons Home Affairs Committee, *Home Office Delivery of Brexit: Immigration* (HC 421, 14 February 2018) [11].

26 This process was tested on a small scale before its launch. See Home Office, *EU Settlement Scheme: Private Beta Testing Phase 1 Report* (31 October 2018); Home Office, *EU Settlement Scheme: Private Beta Testing Phase 2 Report* (21 January 2019). For discussion of this testing, see Independent Chief Inspector of Borders and Immigration, *An Inspection of the EU Settlement Scheme: November 2018–January 2019* (May 2019) [3.1]–[3.10].

27 For further analysis, see A. Welsh and J. Tomlinson, 'Will Digital Immigration Status Work?' (2020) 34(4) *Journal of Immigration, Asylum, and Nationality Law* 306; J. Tomlinson, J. Maxwell, and A. Welsh, 'Discrimination in Digital Immigration Status' (2021) *Legal Studies* (forthcoming).

28 For a detailed technical analysis of how this system works, see P. Booth, *Automated Data Checks in the EU Settlement Scheme* (MedConfidential, 2019).

29 According to the impact assessment produced for the scheme, it is expected to cost the Home Office between £410 million and £460 million, depending on the number and types of applicants. See Home Office, *Impact Assessment for EU Settlement Scheme* (HO 0316, July 2018).

[30] See, e.g., M.L. Gray and S. Suri, *Ghost Work: How to Stop Silicon Valley from Building a New Global Underclass* (Houghton Mifflin Harcourt, 2019). See also: J. Christensen, L. Aarøe, M. Baekgaard, P. Herd, and D.P. Moynihan, 'Human Capital and Administrative Burden: The Role of Cognitive Resources in Citizen-State Interactions' (2020) 80(1) *Public Administration Review* 127.

[31] See, e.g., A. Bryson and R. Berthoud, 'Social Security Appeals: What Do the Claimants Want?' (1997) 4 *Journal of Social Security Law* 17.

[32] House of Lords European Affairs Committee, *Citizens' Rights* (HL Paper 46, 23 July 2021) [57].

[33] J. Tomlinson, 'Justice in Automated Administration' (2020) 40(4) *Oxford Journal of Legal Studies* 708.

[34] M.T. Dzindolet, S.A. Peterson, R.A. Pomranky, L.G. Pierce, and H.P. Beck, 'The Role of Trust in Automation Reliance' (2003) 58(6) *International Journal of Human-Computer Studies* 697.

[35] Open Rights Group and Immigration Law Practitioners' Association, 'EU Settled Status Automated Checks: Proposed Outcomes, Concerns and Questions' (2019).

[36] For a widely read account of key concerns, see V. Eubanks, *Automating Inequality: How High Tech Tools Profile, Police and Punish the Poor* (St. Martin's Press, 2018).

[37] M. Sumption, *Not Settled Yet? Understanding the EU Settlement Scheme Using the Available Data* (The Migration Observatory, 2020).

[38] Independent Chief Inspector of Borders and Immigration, *An Inspection of the EU Settlement Scheme: November 2018–January 2019* (May 2019) [6.28].

[39] Independent Chief Inspector of Borders and Immigration, *An Inspection of the EU Settlement Scheme: November 2018–January 2019* (May 2019) [6.28].

[40] For related concerns, see House of Commons Home Affairs Committee, *Home Office Delivery of Brexit: Immigration* (HC 421, 14 February 2018).

[41] House of Lords European Affairs Committee, *Citizens' Rights* (HL Paper 46, 23 July 2021) [109]–[115].

[42] Independent Chief Inspector of Borders and Immigration, *An Inspection of the EU Settlement Scheme: November 2018–January 2019* (May 2019) [6.40].

[43] Assisted digital services for application were provided in collaboration with an external organization, We Are Digital. This organization then worked with local 'delivery partners' across the UK. For analysis of some of the issues with service provision of this kind, see JUSTICE, *Preventing Digital Exclusion from Online Justice* (2018); Civil Justice Council, *Assisted Digital Support for Civil Justice System Users: Demand, Design, and Implementation* (2018).

[44] *Oakley v South Cambridgeshire DC* [2017] EWCA Civ 71.

45 A. Welsh and J. Tomlinson, 'Will Digital Immigration Status Work?' (2020) 34(4) *Journal of Immigration, Asylum, and Nationality Law* 306; J. Tomlinson, J. Maxwell, and A. Welsh, 'Discrimination in Digital Immigration Status' (2021) *Legal Studies* (forthcoming).

46 House of Lords European Affairs Committee, *Citizens' Rights* (HL Paper 46, 23 July 2021) [92]–[93].

47 M. Lipsky, 'Bureaucratic Disentitlement in Social Welfare Programs' (1984) 58(1) *Social Service Review* 3.

48 For critical analysis of previous attempts to data share for the purposes of immigration administration, see L. Hiam, S. Steele, and M. McKee, 'Creating a "Hostile Environment for Migrants": The British Government's Use of Health Service Data to Restrict Immigration Is a Very Bad Idea' (2018) 13(2) *Health Economics, Policy and Law* 107; Liberty, *Care Don't Share: Why we need a firewall between essential public services and immigration enforcement* (2018).

49 Home Office, *EU Settlement Scheme: Statement of Intent* (21 June 2018) [5.18].

50 Immigration and Social Security Co-ordination (EU Withdrawal) Bill (HC 309).

51 Home Office, *EU Settlement Scheme: Statement of Intent* (2018) [5.19].

52 Home Office, *EU Settlement Scheme: Statement of Intent* (2018) [5.19].

53 Immigration Rules Appendix AR (EU).

54 R. Thomas and J. Tomlinson, 'A Different Tale of Judicial Power: Administrative Review as a Problematic Response to the Judicialisation of Tribunals' [2019] *Public Law* 537.

55 R. Thomas and J. Tomlinson, 'A Different Tale of Judicial Power: Administrative Review as a Problematic Response to the Judicialisation of Tribunals' [2019] *Public Law* 537.

56 Immigration Rules Appendix AR (EU). An application for administrative review comes with an £80 fee.

57 Immigration Rules Appendix AR (EU).

58 *Agreement on the withdrawal of the United Kingdom of Great Britain and Northern Ireland from the European Union and the European Atomic Energy Community, as endorsed by leaders at a special meeting of the European Council on 25 November 2018* (2018) art.21.

59 Home Office, *EU Settlement Scheme: Statement of Intent* (2018) [5.19].

60 Department for Exiting the European Union, *Citizens' Rights – EU citizens in the UK and UK nationals in the EU* (2018) [9].

61 Department for Exiting the European Union, *Citizens' Rights – EU citizens in the UK and UK nationals in the EU* (2018) [11].

62 European Union (Withdrawal Agreement) Bill 2019-20 cl.11.

63 European Union (Withdrawal Agreement) Act 2020 s.11.

64 The Immigration (Citizens' Rights Appeals) (EU Exit) Regulations 2020, SI 2020/61.

four Category Errors

1   R.N. Pailey, *Written Evidence Submission to All-Party Parliamentary Group on Africa* (January 2019); All-Party Parliamentary Group for Africa, *Visa Problems for African Visitors to the UK* (July 2019) 25–6.

2   R.N. Pailey, *Written Evidence Submission to All-Party Parliamentary Group on Africa* (January 2019); All-Party Parliamentary Group for Africa, *Visa Problems for African Visitors to the UK* (July 2019) 25–6.

3   J. Hampshire, 'The Future of Border Control: Risk Management of Migration in the UK', in H. Fassmann, M. Haller, and D. Lane (eds), *Migration and Mobility in Europe: Trends, Patterns and Control* (Edward Elgar, 2009) 229.

4   Immigration Act 1971 s.3.

5   Immigration Act 1971 s.3(2).

6   In 2018, for example, there were 142.9 million passenger arrivals in the UK, of which 81.7 million (57 per cent) were returning British citizens, 40.8 million (29 per cent) other EEA nationals and 20.4 million (14 per cent) from outside the EEA. See Home Office and Office for National Statistics, *Immigration Statistics: year ending December 2020* (25 February 2021).

7   See J. Hampshire, 'The Future of Border Control: Risk Management of Migration in the UK', in H. Fassmann, M. Haller, and D. Lane (eds), *Migration and Mobility in Europe: Trends, Patterns and Control* (Edward Elgar, 2009) 236.

8   For example of the language of 'immigration risk', see HM Government, *The UK's Future Skills-based Immigration System* (Cm 9722, December 2018) [4.23]. A person can only claim asylum from a country once they are physically present in that country.

9   Home Office, 'Government expands use of ePassport gates to 7 more countries' (20 May 2019) <www.gov.uk/government/news/government-expands-use-of-epassport-gates-to-7-more-countries>.

10 Immigration Rules paras 24–30C.

11 See, e.g., Independent Chief Inspector of Borders and Immigration, *An Inspection of Entry Clearance Processing Operations in Croydon and Istanbul: November 2016–March 2017* (July 2017) fig. 3; Independent Chief Inspector of Borders and Immigration, *An Inspection of the Home Office's Network Consolidation Programme and the 'Onshoring' of Visa Processing and Decision Making to the UK: September 2018–August 2019* (February 2020) [5.9]–[5.15].

12 Over 95 per cent of visa applications are electronic, rather than paper-based. See Independent Chief Inspector of Borders and Immigration, *An Inspection of the Home Office's Network Consolidation Programme and the 'Onshoring' of Visa Processing and Decision Making to the UK: September 2018–August 2019* (February 2020) [5.14]. Certain groups of applicants can use the 'UK Immigration: ID Check' smartphone app to submit this information.

13 Until 2008, the Home Office operated over 100 of these centres around the world, but it has since consolidated and 'onshored' this process, due to the advent of online applications and lower operating costs in the UK. As a result, many entry clearance applications are now decided by officials in the UK. See generally Independent Chief Inspector of Borders and Immigration, *An Inspection of the Home Office's Network Consolidation Programme and the 'Onshoring' of Visa Processing and Decision Making to the UK: September 2018–August 2019* (February 2020).

14 Proof of entry clearance usually comes in the form of a visa, which has effect as leave to enter. See Immigration Rules paras 25–25A; Immigration (Leave to Enter and Remain) Order 2000, SI 2000/1161.

15 See generally B. Ryan, 'Extraterritorial Immigration Control: What Role for Legal Guarantees?' in B. Ryan and V. Mitsilegas (eds), *Extraterritorial Immigration Control: Legal Challenges* (Brill, 2010) 3; G. Clayton, 'The UK and Extraterritorial Immigration Control: Entry Clearance and Juxtaposed Control' in B. Ryan and V. Mitsilegas (eds), *Extraterritorial Immigration Control: Legal Challenges* (Brill, 2010) 397.

16 HC Deb, 3 June 1985, vol 80 col 52.

17 Immigration Rules Appendix Visitor para VN1.1.

18 For an analysis of how visa policies have tended to foster inequality between the Global North and the Global South, see S. Mau, F. Gülzau, L. Laube, and N. Zaun, 'The Global Mobility Divide: How Visa Policies Have Evolved over Time' (2015) 41 *Journal of Ethnic and Migration Studies* 1192.

19 Home Office, *Securing the UK Border: Our Vision and Strategy for the Future* (March 2007) [3.5].

20 P. De Hert and R. Bellanova, *Transatlantic Cooperation on Travelers' Data Processing: From Sorting Countries to Sorting Individuals* (Migration Policy Institute and European University Institute, March 2011).

21 E. Smith and M. Marmo, *Race, Gender and the Body in British Immigration Control: Subject to Examination* (Palgrave, 2014).

22 Commission for Racial Equality, *Immigration Control Procedure: Report of a Formal Investigation* (February 1985) [2.5.3].

23 Commission for Racial Equality, *Immigration Control Procedure: Report of a Formal Investigation* (February 1985) [2.4.1]–[2.4.14].

24 Commission for Racial Equality, *Immigration Control Procedure: Report of a Formal Investigation* (February 1985) [2.5.6].

25 Commission for Racial Equality, *Immigration Control Procedure: Report of a Formal Investigation* (February 1985) [2.5.9], [6.20.4], [11.10.1]. See also [11.6.14].

26 Commission for Racial Equality, *Immigration Control Procedure: Report of a Formal Investigation* (February 1985) [6.20.4]. See also [11.6.15].

27 Commission for Racial Equality, *Immigration Control Procedure: Report of a Formal Investigation* (February 1985) [2.5.8]–[2.5.9].

28 National Audit Office, *Visa Entry to the United Kingdom: The Entry Clearance Operation* (HC 367, 17 June 2004) [2.6].

29 National Audit Office, *Visa Entry to the United Kingdom: The Entry Clearance Operation* (HC 367, 17 June 2004) [2.11].

30 Independent Chief Inspector of Borders and Immigration, *A Comparative Inspection of the UK Border Agency Visa Sections that Process Applications Submitted in Africa: Nairobi, Abuja, Pretoria and the UK Visa Section: May–July 2011* (June 2012) [4.131]; Independent Chief Inspector of Borders and Immigration, *A Short-notice Inspection of Decision-making Quality in the Warsaw Visa Section: 23–27 September 2013* (December 2013) [4.23].

31 Independent Chief Inspector of Borders and Immigration, *A Short-notice Inspection of the Amman Visa Section: March 2015* (October 2015) [5.2].

32 Independent Chief Inspector of Borders and Immigration, *A Short-notice Inspection of Decision-making Quality in the Warsaw Visa Section: 23–27 September 2013* (December 2013) [4.22]–[4.40].

33 Independent Chief Inspector of Borders and Immigration, *An Inspection of the Risk and Liaison Overseas Network (RALON) in Islamabad and the United Arab Emirates: January–April 2010* (November 2010) [5.6], [5.10], [5.29]–[5.38].

34 Independent Chief Inspector of Borders and Immigration, *A Short-notice Inspection of Decision-making Quality in the Warsaw Visa Section: 23–27 September 2013* (December 2013) [4.29]–[4.34].

35 Independent Chief Inspector of Borders and Immigration, *An Inspection of the Risk and Liaison Overseas Network (RALON) in Islamabad and the United Arab Emirates: January–April 2010* (November 2010) [5.4]; Independent Chief Inspector of Borders and Immigration, *A Comparative Inspection of the UK Border Agency Visa Sections that Process Applications Submitted in Africa: Nairobi, Abuja, Pretoria and the UK Visa Section: May–July 2011* (June 2012) [4.142]; Independent Chief Inspector of Borders and Immigration, *A Short-notice Inspection of Decision-making Quality in the Warsaw Visa Section: 23–27 September 2013* (December 2013) [4.28]; Independent Chief Inspector of Borders and Immigration, *A Short-notice Inspection of Decision-making Quality in the Paris Visa Section: 10–13 June 2014* (October 2014) [4.42].

36 Independent Chief Inspector of Borders and Immigration, *A Short-notice Inspection of Decision-making Quality in the Warsaw Visa Section: 23–27 September 2013* (December 2013) [4.28], [4.38].

37 Independent Chief Inspector of Borders and Immigration, *An Inspection of Family Visitor Visa Applications: August–December 2014* (July 2015) [6.7]; Independent Chief Inspector of Borders and Immigration, *An Inspection of Entry Clearance Processing Operations in Croydon and Istanbul: November 2016–March 2017* (July 2017) [7.3].

38 See Home Office, *Data Protection Impact Assessment* (21 January 2020).

39 Between 2010 and 2019, there was a 43 per cent increase in the number of entry clearance applications. See Home Office and Office of National Statistics, *Immigration Statistics: Year Ending December 2021* (25 February 2021) table Vis_D01.

40 See Independent Chief Inspector of Borders and Immigration, *An Inspection of Entry Clearance Processing Operations in Croydon and Istanbul: November 2016–March 2017* (July 2017) [7.7].

41 Home Office, *Data Protection Impact Assessment* (21 January 2020) 8.

42 See generally Independent Chief Inspector of Borders and Immigration, *An Inspection of Entry Clearance Processing Operations in Croydon and Istanbul: November 2016–March 2017* (July 2017) [7.3]–[7.14]; Independent Chief Inspector of Borders and Immigration, *An Inspection of the Home Office's Network Consolidation Programme and the 'Onshoring' of Visa Processing and Decision Making to the UK* (February 2020) [7.20]–[7.33]; Claimant's Statement of Facts and Grounds for Judicial Review, *R (Joint Council for the Welfare of Immigrants) v Secretary of State for the Home Department* (4 June 2020) <drive.google.com/file/d/12WzweATsBzrjUjuC7bXSH8_YcSyPb1a_/view>.

43 Home Office, *Equality Act, Nationality Risk Assessment (April 2019–June 2019); For the Ministerial Authorisation under Paragraph 17 of Schedule 3 of the Equality Act 2010* (October 2019).

44 Home Office, *Equality Act, Nationality Risk Assessment (April 2019–June 2019); For the Ministerial Authorisation under Paragraph 17 of Schedule 3 of the Equality Act 2010* (October 2019).

45 Home Office, *Standardisation: Streaming, Enrichment & Operational Review Meetings (ORMs)* (October 2017).

46 See generally Independent Chief Inspector of Borders and Immigration, *An Inspection of Entry Clearance Processing Operations in Croydon and Istanbul: November 2016–March 2017* (July 2017) [7.3]–[7.14]; Independent Chief Inspector of Borders and Immigration, *An Inspection of the Home Office's Network Consolidation Programme and the 'Onshoring' of Visa Processing and Decision Making to the UK* (February 2020) [7.20]–[7.33]; Claimant's Statement of Facts and Grounds for

Judicial Review, *R (Joint Council for the Welfare of Immigrants) v Secretary of State for the Home Department* (4 June 2020) <drive.google.com/file/d/12WzweATsBzrjUjuC7bXSH8_YcSyPb1a_/view>.

47 Home Office, *Standard Operating Procedures: AO Grade Decision Makers* (November 2017); Independent Chief Inspector of Borders and Immigration, *An Inspection of the Home Office's Network Consolidation Programme and the 'Onshoring' of Visa Processing and Decision Making to the UK* (February 2020) [7.27].

48 Home Office, *Standardisation: Streaming, Enrichment & Operational Review Meetings (ORMs)* (October 2017) 3–6.

49 National Audit Office, *Digital Services at the Border* (HC 1069, 9 December 2020) [1.5].

50 These benchmarks are for visitor visas. See Independent Chief Inspector of Borders and Immigration, *An Inspection of the Home Office's Network Consolidation Programme and the 'Onshoring' of Visa Processing and Decision Making to the UK* (February 2020) fig. 15.

51 Home Office, *Review to Risk Matrix* (3 April 2017).

52 Independent Chief Inspector of Borders and Immigration, *An Inspection of Entry Clearance Processing Operations in Croydon and Istanbul: November 2016–March 2017* (July 2017) [9.32].

53 Independent Chief Inspector of Borders and Immigration, *An Inspection of Entry Clearance Processing Operations in Croydon and Istanbul: November 2016–March 2017* (July 2017) [7.12]. See also Independent Chief Inspector of Borders and Immigration, *An Inspection of the Home Office's Network Consolidation Programme and the 'Onshoring' of Visa Processing and Decision Making to the UK* (February 2020) [7.26].

54 For visitor applications from Africa. See Independent Chief Inspector of Borders and Immigration, *An Inspection of the Home Office's Network Consolidation Programme and the 'Onshoring' of Visa Processing and Decision Making to the UK* (February 2020) [7.26].

55 HC Deb, 19 June 2019, vol 662 cols 322–4.

56 National Audit Office, *Visa Entry to the United Kingdom: The Entry Clearance Operation* (HC 367, 17 June 2004) fig. 5. See also All-Party Parliamentary Group for Africa, *Visa Problems for African Visitors to the UK* (July 2019).

57 HC Deb, 19 June 2019, vol 662 cols 322–4.

58 See All-Party Parliamentary Group for Africa, *Visa Problems for African Visitors to the UK* (July 2019) 8.

59 See, e.g., Centre for Data Ethics and Innovation, *Review into Bias in Algorithmic Decision-making* (November 2020).

60 Equality Act 2010 s.31(10), sch 3 para 17.

61 *Ghaidan v Godin-Mendoza* [2004] UKHL 30 [9].

62   *R (European Roma Rights Centre) v Immigration Officer at Prague Airport* [2004] UKHL 55 [82] (citations omitted).

63   HC Deb, 29 April 2014, c660W.

64   National Audit Office, *Immigration Enforcement* (HC 110, 17 June 2020) [1.14]–[1.18].

65   Independent Chief Inspector of Borders and Immigration, *An Inspection of the Intelligence Functions of Border Force and Immigration Enforcement* (July 2016) [6.6]–[6.11]; National Audit Office, *Immigration Enforcement* (HC 110, 17 June 2020) [2.17].

66   Independent Chief Inspector of Borders and Immigration, *An Inspection of How the Home Office Tackles Illegal Working* (December 2015) [1.10], [5.46]. See also Independent Chief Inspector of Borders and Immigration, *An Inspection of the Home Office's Approach to Illegal Working: August–December 2018* (May 2019) [9.30].

67   National Audit Office, *Immigration Enforcement* (HC 110, 17 June 2020) fig. 9.

68   Independent Chief Inspector of Borders and Immigration, *An Inspection of the Home Office's Approach to Illegal Working: August–December 2018* (May 2019) [8.21]–[8.22].

69   D. Ensign, S.A. Friedler, S. Neville, C. Scheidegger, and S. Venkatasubramanian, 'Runaway Feedback Loops in Predictive Policing' (2018) 81 *Proceedings of Machine Learning Research* 1.

70   Data Protection Act 2018 s.64(1).

71   Data Protection Act 2018 s.64(3).

72   See S.L. Harris, 'Data Protection Impact Assessments as Rule of Law Governance Mechanisms' (2020) 2 *Data and Policy* e2.

73   Home Office, *Data Protection Impact Assessment* (21 January 2020) [3.1], [4.16].

74   Home Office, *Data Protection Impact Assessment* (21 January 2020) [4.11].

75   L.J. Skitka, K.L. Mosier, and M. Burdick, 'Does Automation Bias Decision-making?' (1999) 51 *International Journal of Human-Computer Studies* 991.

76   See, e.g., *Lavender v Minister of Housing and Local Government* [1970] 1 WLR 1231; *British Oxygen Co Ltd v Minister of Technology* [1971] AC 610.

77   See, e.g., Regulation (EU) 2016/679 arts 13(2)(f), 14(2)(g), 15(1)(h), 22.

78   Home Office, 'Home Office in the media: Wednesday 30 October' (30 October 2019) <homeofficemedia.blog.gov.uk/2019/10/30/7013>.

79   HC Deb, 19 June 2019, vol 662 col 323.

80   See generally Independent Chief Inspector of Borders and Immigration, *An Inspection of Entry Clearance Processing Operations in Croydon and Istanbul: November 2016–March 2017* (July 2017) [3.7], [7.10]–[7.11]; Independent Chief Inspector of Borders and Immigration, *An Inspection*

of the Home Office's Network Consolidation Programme and the 'Onshoring' of Visa Processing and Decision Making to the UK (February 2020) [3.15]–[3.17], [7.26].

81 M. Rovatsos, B. Mittelstadt, and A. Koene, *Landscape Summary: Bias in Algorithmic Decision-Making* (Centre for Data Ethics and Innovation, July 2019) 48.

82 Home Office, *Standardisation: Streaming, Enrichment & Operational Review Meetings (ORMs)* (October 2017) 5.

83 Independent Chief Inspector of Borders and Immigration, *An Inspection of Entry Clearance Processing Operations in Croydon and Istanbul: November 2016–March 2017* (July 2017) [7.11]. It appears that officials have used risk ratings to justify their decisions in this way for some time. See, e.g., Independent Chief Inspector of the UK Border Agency, *An Inspection of the UK Border Agency Visa Section in Amman, Jordan: August–October 2010* (March 2011) [5.34]; Independent Chief Inspector of Borders and Immigration, *An Inspection of Family Visitor Visa Applications: August–December 2014* (July 2015) [5.61]–[5.63].

84 R. Thomas, 'Immigration Appeals for Family Visitors Refused Entry Clearance' [2004] *Public Law* 612, 617.

85 R. Thomas, 'Immigration Appeals for Family Visitors Refused Entry Clearance' [2004] *Public Law* 612, 617.

86 Independent Chief Inspector of Borders and Immigration, *An Inspection of Entry Clearance Processing Operations in Croydon and Istanbul: November 2016–March 2017* (July 2017) [8.4].

87 Independent Chief Inspector of Borders and Immigration, *An Inspection of the Home Office's Network Consolidation Programme and the 'Onshoring' of Visa Processing and Decision Making to the UK* (February 2020) [7.80].

88 Independent Chief Inspector of Borders and Immigration, *An Inspection of the Home Office's Network Consolidation Programme and the 'Onshoring' of Visa Processing and Decision Making to the UK* (February 2020) [7.85].

89 K. Goddard, A. Roudsari, and J.C. Wyatt, 'Automation Bias: A Systematic Review of Frequency, Effect Mediators, and Mitigators' (2011) 19 *Journal of the American Medical Informatics Association* 121.

90 For visitor applications from Africa. See Independent Chief Inspector of Borders and Immigration, *An Inspection of the Home Office's Network Consolidation Programme and the 'Onshoring' of Visa Processing and Decision Making to the UK* (February 2020) [7.26].

91 Independent Chief Inspector of Borders and Immigration, *An Inspection of the Home Office's Network Consolidation Programme and the 'Onshoring' of Visa Processing and Decision Making to the UK* (February 2020) [7.28], [7.84].

[92] Independent Chief Inspector of Borders and Immigration, *An Inspection of the Home Office's Network Consolidation Programme and the 'Onshoring' of Visa Processing and Decision Making to the UK* (February 2020) [3.17].

[93] There is a growing body of empirical research into the factors that reinforce and mitigate automation bias. See, e.g., R. Parasuraman and D.H. Manzey, 'Complacency and Bias in Human Use of Automation: An Attentional Integration' (2010) 52 *Human Factors* 381; K. Goddard, A. Roudsari, and J.C. Wyatt, 'Automation Bias: A Systematic Review of Frequency, Effect Mediators, and Mitigators' (2011) 19 *Journal of the American Medical Informatics Association* 121.

[94] Independent Chief Inspector of Borders and Immigration, *An Inspection of Entry Clearance Processing Operations in Croydon and Istanbul: November 2016–March 2017* (July 2017) [3.7].

[95] Home Office, *Data Protection Impact Assessment* (21 January 2020) [4.1], [4.12].

[96] Home Office, *Data Protection Impact Assessment* (21 January 2020) [4.17].

[97] Independent Chief Inspector of Borders and Immigration, *An Inspection of Family Visitor Visa Applications: August–December 2014* (July 2015) [6.7]; Independent Chief Inspector of Borders and Immigration, *An Inspection of Entry Clearance Processing Operations in Croydon and Istanbul: November 2016–March 2017* (July 2017) [7.3]–[7.14], fig. 5.

[98] Independent Chief Inspector of Borders and Immigration, *An Inspection of the Home Office's Network Consolidation Programme and the 'Onshoring' of Visa Processing and Decision Making to the UK* (February 2020) [4.4].

[99] Home Office, *The Home Office Response to the Independent Chief Inspector of Borders and Immigration's Report: An Inspection of the Home Office's Network Consolidation Programme and the 'Onshoring' of Visa Processing and Decision Making to the UK* (February 2020) [4.3].

[100] See, e.g., UK Visas and Immigration, *Guidance: Visit visa: guide to supporting documents* (18 January 2021).

[101] See, e.g., Independent Chief Inspector of the UK Border Agency, *An Inspection of the UK Border Agency Visa Section in Amman, Jordan: August–October 2010* (March 2011) [5.11]; Independent Chief Inspector of Borders and Immigration, *An Inspection of the UK Visas & Immigration Visa Section in Dhaka: April–July 2013* (December 2013) [4.34]–[4.35]; All-Party Parliamentary Group for Africa, *Visa Problems for African Visitors to the UK* (July 2019) 26–7.

[102] All-Party Parliamentary Group for Africa, *Visa Problems for African Visitors to the UK* (July 2019) 27.

[103] All-Party Parliamentary Group for Africa, *Visa Problems for African Visitors to the UK* (July 2019) 27.

104 See, e.g., Independent Chief Inspector of the UK Border Agency, *An Inspection of the UK Border Agency Visa Section in Amman, Jordan: August–October 2010* (March 2011) [5.11]; Independent Chief Inspector of Borders and Immigration, *An Inspection of the UK Visas & Immigration Visa Section in Dhaka: April–July 2013* (December 2013) [4.34]–[4.35].

105 H. Warrell, 'Home Office under fire for using secretive visa algorithm' (*Financial Times*, 9 June 2019) <www.ft.com/content/0206dd56-87b0-11e9-a028-86cea8523dc2>.

106 HC Deb, 19 June 2019, vol 662 cols 316–21.

107 Independent Chief Inspector of Borders and Immigration, *An Inspection of the Home Office's Network Consolidation Programme and the 'Onshoring' of Visa Processing and Decision Making to the UK* (February 2020) [3.15]. See also All-Party Parliamentary Group for Africa, *Visa Problems for African Visitors to the UK* (July 2019) 21–2.

108 All-Party Parliamentary Group for Africa, *Visa Problems for African Visitors to the UK* (July 2019) 24.

109 R. Thomas, 'Immigration Appeals for Family Visitors Refused Entry Clearance' [2004] *Public Law* 612, 620.

110 See B. Ryan, 'Extraterritorial Immigration Control: What Role for Legal Guarantees?' in B. Ryan and V. Mitsilegas (eds), *Extraterritorial Immigration Control: Legal Challenges* (Brill, 2010) 3.

111 In general, tribunal appeals are only available in respect of human rights and asylum claims, following the Immigration Act 2014 and Immigration Act 2016.

112 For example, applicants for visitor visas, the single largest category of applicants, are not eligible for administrative review. They are simply expected to make another application.

113 In 2020, the Independent Chief Inspector of Borders and Immigration estimated that around 5,000 people per year seek administrative review of out-of-country entry clearance decisions. See Independent Chief Inspector of Borders and Immigration, *An Inspection of Administrative Reviews (May–December 2019)* (May 2020) [7.79].

114 Independent Chief Inspector of Borders and Immigration, *An Inspection of Administrative Reviews (May–December 2019)* (May 2020) [7.79]. In general, administrative reviews have tended to have a lower overturn rate than other redress mechanisms, such as tribunal appeals. See, e.g., National Audit Office, *Visa Entry to the United Kingdom: The Entry Clearance Operation* (HC 367, 17 June 2004) [2.24], [2.28].

115 H. McDonald, 'AI system for granting UK visas is biased, rights groups claim' (*The Guardian*, 29 October 2019) <www.theguardian.com/uk-news/2019/oct/29/ai-system-for-granting-uk-visas-is-biased-rights-groups-claim>.

116 Foxglove, 'About', <www.foxglove.org.uk/about>.

117 Letter from Treasury Solicitor to Rosa Curling (3 August 2020) <drive. google.com/file/d/1XfkKPT3JYlgzfa6tovppFf5VXVefwEVY/view>.

118 See, e.g., L. Edwards and M. Veale, 'Slave to the Algorithm? Why a 'Right to an Explanation' Is Probably Not the Remedy You Are Looking For' (2017) 16 *Duke Law and Technology Review* 18, 74–5.

119 M. Kaminski, 'Binary Governance: Lessons from the GDPR's Approach to Algorithmic Accountability' (2019) 92 *Southern California Law Review* 1529, 1558.

120 See generally M. Galanter, 'Why the "Haves" Come Out Ahead: Speculations on the Limits of Legal Change' (1974) 9 *Law and Society Review* 95.

121 See Ministry of Justice, 'Pre-Action Protocol for Judicial Review' (17 September 2019).

122 Treasury Solicitor's Department, *Guidance on Discharging the Duty of Candour and Disclosure in Judicial Review Proceedings* (January 2010).

123 See the references in Claimant's Statement of Facts and Grounds for Judicial Review, *R (Joint Council for the Welfare of Immigrants) v Secretary of State for the Home Department* (4 June 2020) <drive.google.com/file/ d/12WzweATsBzrjUjuC7bXSH8_YcSyPb1a_/view>.

124 Claimant's Statement of Facts and Grounds for Judicial Review, *R (Joint Council for the Welfare of Immigrants) v Secretary of State for the Home Department* (4 June 2020) <drive.google.com/file/d/ 12WzweATsBzrjUjuC7bXSH8_YcSyPb1a_/view>.

125 See, e.g., *Rooke's Case* (1598) 5 Co.Rep. 99b.

126 Claimant's Statement of Facts and Grounds for Judicial Review, *R (Joint Council for the Welfare of Immigrants) v Secretary of State for the Home Department* (4 June 2020) <drive.google.com/file/d/ 12WzweATsBzrjUjuC7bXSH8_YcSyPb1a_/view>.

127 Letter from Treasury Solicitor to Rosa Curling (3 August 2020) <drive. google.com/file/d/1XfkKPT3JYlgzfa6tovppFf5VXVefwEVY/view>.

128 M. Kaminski, 'Binary Governance: Lessons from the GDPR's Approach to Algorithmic Accountability' (2019) 92 *Southern California Law Review* 1529, 1558.

129 See, e.g., Independent Chief Inspector of Borders and Immigration, *The Implementation of the 2014 'Hostile Environment' Provisions for Tackling Sham Marriage: August to September 2016* (December 2016) [7.4]–[7.16]; Home Office, *Equality Impact Assessment* (30 November 2020); Independent Chief Inspector of Borders and Immigration, *An Inspection of Border Force's Identification and Treatment of Potential Victims of Modern Slavery: July to October 2016* (February 2017) [9.2]; National Audit Office, *Digital Services at the Border* (HC 1069, 9 December 2020).

five Precautionary Measures

1 See P. Molnar, 'Technology on the Margins: AI and Global Migration Management from a Human Rights Perspective' (2019) 8(2) *Cambridge International Law Journal* 305, 325–8.

2 P. Molnar, *Technological Testing Grounds: Migration Management Experiments and Reflections from the Ground Up* (EDRi and Refugee Law Lab, 2020) 3.

3 J. Tomlinson, *Justice in the Digital State: Assessing the Next Revolution in Administrative Justice* (Bristol University Press, 2019).

4 G. Teubner, 'Juridification: Concepts, Aspects, Limits, Solutions' in G. Teubner (ed), *Juridification of Social Spheres: A Comparative Analysis in the Areas of Labor, Corporate, Antitrust, and Social Welfare Law* (Walter de Gruyter, 1987).

5 J.L. Mashaw, 'Structuring a Dense Complexity: Accountability and the Project of Administrative Law' (2005) 5(1) *Issues in Legal Scholarship* 1, 14.

6 J.L. Mashaw, 'Structuring a Dense Complexity: Accountability and the Project of Administrative Law' (2005) 5(1) *Issues in Legal Scholarship* 1, 14.

7 J.L. Mashaw, *Bureaucratic Justice: Managing Social Security Disability Claims* (Yale University Press, 1983).

8 J. Cobbe, M. Seng Ah Lee, H. Janssen, and J. Singh, 'Centering the Law in the Digital State' (2020) 53(10) *Computer* 47.

9 M. Lipsky, *Street Level Bureaucracy: Dilemmas of the Individual in Public Services* (Russell Sage, 1980); B. Zacka, *When the State Meets Street* (Harvard University Press, 2017).

10 See generally on the role of digital design: J. Tomlinson, *Justice in the Digital State: Assessing the Next Revolution in Administrative Justice* (Bristol University Press, 2019), ch. 4; A. Clarke and J. Craft, 'The Twin Faces of Public Sector Design' (2018) 32 *Governance* 5; A. Clarke and J. Craft, 'The Vestiges and Vanguards of Policy Design in a Digital Context' (2017) 60(4) *Canadian Public Administration* 476.

11 *Report of the Special Rapporteur on extreme poverty and human rights* (A/74/493, 11 October 2019).

12 S. Ranchordas and M. van 't Schip, 'Future-Proofing Legislation for the Digital Age' in S. Ranchordas and Y. Roznai (eds), *Time, Law, and Change* (Hart, 2020).

13 J. Cobbe, M. Seng Ah Lee, H. Janssen, and J. Singh, 'Centering the Law in the Digital State' (2020) 53(10) *Computer* 47.

14 M. Adler, 'Constructing a Typology of Administrative Grievances: Reconciling the Irreconcilable?' in R. Banakar and M. Travers (eds), *Theory and Method in Socio-Legal Research* (Hart, 2005) 287–8.

15 M. Adler, 'Constructing a Typology of Administrative Grievances: Reconciling the Irreconcilable?' in R. Banakar and M. Travers (eds), *Theory and Method in Socio-Legal Research* (Hart, 2005) 288.

16 M. Adler, 'Constructing a Typology of Administrative Grievances: Reconciling the Irreconcilable?' in R. Banakar and M. Travers (eds), *Theory and Method in Socio-Legal Research* (Hart, 2005) 289.

17 J. Tomlinson, 'Justice in Automated Administration' (2020) 40(4) *Oxford Journal of Legal Studies* 708.

18 R. Binns, M. Van Kleek, M. Veale, U. Lyngs, J. Zhao, and N. Shadbolt, ' "It's Reducing a Human Being to a Percentage": Perceptions of Justice in Algorithmic Decisions' (2018) *Proceedings of the 2018 CHI Conference on Human Factors in Computing Systems*, https://doi.org/10.1145/3173 574.3173951. See also J. Tasioulas, 'First Steps Towards an Ethics of Robots and Artificial Intelligence' (2019) 7(1) *Journal of Practical Ethics* 61, 75–81.

19 R. Binns, M. Van Kleek, M. Veale, U. Lyngs, J. Zhao, and N. Shadbolt, ' "It's Reducing a Human Being to a Percentage": Perceptions of Justice in Algorithmic Decisions' (2018) *Proceedings of the 2018 CHI Conference on Human Factors in Computing Systems*, https://doi.org/10.1145/3173 574.3173951. See also R. Binns, 'Human Judgment in Algorithmic Loops: Individual Justice and Automated Decision-making' (2020) *Regulation and Governance*, https://doi.org/10.1111/rego.12358

20 See, e.g., J. King, *Judging Social Rights* (Cambridge University Press, 2012) ch. 3.

21 V. Bondy and A. Le Sueur, *Designing Redress: A Study About Grievances Against Public Bodies* (Public Law Project, 2012).

22 V. Bondy and A. Le Sueur, *Designing Redress: A Study About Grievances Against Public Bodies* (Public Law Project, 2012). See also D. Cowan, A. Dymond, S. Halliday, and C. Hunter, 'Reconsidering Mandatory Reconsideration' [2017] *Public Law* 215.

23 T. O'Riordan and J. Cameron (eds), *Interpreting the Precautionary Principle* (Routledge, 1994).

24 *R (Langton) v Secretary of State for Environment, Food and Rural Affairs* [2019] EWCA Civ 1562 [53].

25 *R (EU Lotto Ltd) v Secretary of State for Digital, Culture, Media and Sport* [2018] EWHC 3111 (Admin) [89].

26 Even the foundational works on the modern state reflect this. See, e.g., T. Hobbes, *Leviathan* (first published 1651, Penguin 2019).

27 See, e.g., E. Fisher, *Risk Regulation and Administrative Constitutionalism* (Hart, 2010). More widely, see U. Beck, *Risk Society: Towards a New Modernity* (SAGE, 1992).

28 There is a broad literature critiquing the principle. See, e.g., C. Sunstein, *Laws of Fear: Beyond the Precautionary Principle* (Cambridge University Press, 2009).

29 N.A. Manson, 'Formulating the Precautionary Principle' (2002) 24 *Environmental Ethics* 263; J. Hughes, 'How Not to Criticize the Precautionary Principle' (2006) 31 *Journal of Medicine and Philosophy* 447.

Index

References to tables appear in **bold** type.
References to endnotes show both the
page number and the note number (108n93).

Ingram Content Group UK Ltd.
Milton Keynes UK
UKHW020030050523
421270UK00004B/314